Praise for *Hunger*

T0269696

"In the world we live in which is full o
book is a breath of fresh air on a subjec
righteousness. People today are indeed hungry and thirsty to learn from people
that lived righteous lives and Phoebe has chosen as examples for us that are
perhaps hidden from the Western reader.... I highly recommend this book
which is full of wisdom and takes a practical and engaging approach to write
about what may otherwise be a weighty subject."

His Grace Bishop Suriel, Professor at Pope Shenouda III
Coptic Orthodox Theological Seminary and author of
Habib Girgis: Coptic Orthodox Educator and a Light in the Darkness

"Farag Mikhail reminds us that fasting is about so much more than just
food ... it is above all, perhaps surprisingly, about intimate union with God. All
intimacy begins with a deep yearning or desire, hunger. Being hungry or thirsty
is a movement of ascent, a point of departure from which we learn to hunger
and thirst for righteousness, or more properly speaking, the Righteous One. This
beautiful book acts as a guide through this hunger in Lent, gently intensifying
week by week our yearning for God."

Rev. Assoc. Professor Daniel Fanous, St Cyril's Coptic Orthodox
Theological College, Sydney, Australia, author of *A Silent Patriarch*

"Phoebe Farag Mikhail's book will join the ranks of Alexander Schmemann's
Great Lent: Journey to Pascha and Thomas Hopko's *Lenten Spring* as fitting
devotional reading from an Orthodox writer. Farag Mikhail has gifted us by
weaving together important ideas from scripture, excerpts from the Church
Fathers, contemporary Orthodox and other Christian writers into a rich tapestry
that reveals Christ. The rich description of the history and practices of the
Coptic Orthodox Church alone is worth the price of entry. But Farag Mikhail's
gift as a writer of Christian living shines through mostly in the practical advice
on practicing righteousness."

Fr. Sujit Thomas, St. Thomas Indian Orthodox Church of Philadelphia

"Farag Mikhail transports the reader to a journey beyond Pascha, a journey
to live as Christians throughout the year. She invites the reader to accompany
her, through her personal reflections, to reflect on the world we live in through
Christian eyes. She invites the reader to make pilgrimage to holy sites and
ideas. *Hunger for Righteousness* is an engaging book and accessible writing. It
is a good read."

Mother Lois, Professor Emerita of History of Early Christianity,
and author of *Balance of the Heart: Desert Spirituality
for Twenty-First-Century Christians*

"Farag Mikhail draws on a broad knowledge of history and literature, enriched by an intimate understanding of the Coptic tradition to offer wisdom and practical help. She lights the route to the proper posture of our Lenten journey using the thread of stories to proclaim the message of grace and the reminder that God works in our imperfections, our humility, our discomfort, our thirst, our hunger."

Sherry Shenoda, author of *Mummy Eaters* and *The Lightkeeper: A Novel*

"Phoebe's work is a poignant way to experience the days leading up to Easter. Where we hunger and thirst for righteousness, here is one way to be filled and guided."

Lisa Colón DeLay, host of *Spark My Muse* podcast
and author of *The Wild Land Within*

"What is remarkable about Phoebe's newest book is its ability to serve as an inspirational theological treatise, a self-help guide (in the best possible sense) and an actionable roadmap for every Christian wishing to thrive from their Lenten journey.... The chapters are rich with content but concise, the prose is lyrical and profound.... God bless Phoebe and reward her for writing this gem destined to become a classic of the Orthodox tradition."

Mireille Mishriky, author of the *Philo and the SuperHolies* series

"This new book ... is a must-read for Christians looking to connect the lives of the saints with their own modern-day struggles."

Laura Michael, author and creator at *Coptic Dad and Mom*

"Phoebe Farag Mikhail has written a tremendously insightful travel guide to help Christians of any tradition ascend the ancient slopes of Lent with purpose, endurance, and resurrectional hope."

Nicole M. Roccas, PhD, Certified trauma-informed coach
and author of *Time and Despondency*

"At last, a book designed for Lent for people living in the world with their families. Farag Mikhail, as in all her writing, is eminently pastoral, widely read, balanced, and practical. I highly recommend it for individual and group study."

Dr. Patricia Fann Bouteneff, President and Founder of Axia Women

Hunger
for RIGHTEOUSNESS

Hunger
for RIGHTEOUSNESS

A Lenten Journey Towards Intimacy with God
and Loving Our Neighbor

Phoebe Farag Mikhail

PARACLETE PRESS
Brewster, Massachusetts

2025 First Printing

Hunger for Righteousness: A Lenten Journey Towards Intimacy with God and Loving Our Neighbor

ISBN 978-1-64060-934-1
Text copyright © 2025 by Phoebe Farag Mikhail
Illustrations by George Makary: copyright © 2025 by Paraclete Press

The Paraclete Press name and logo (dove on cross) are trademarks of Paraclete Press.

Library of Congress Control Number: 2024945661

10 9 8 7 6 5 4 3 2 1

Published by Paraclete Press
Brewster, Massachusetts
www.paracletepress.com

Printed in the United States of America

CONTENTS

To my mother-in-law,
Wedad Gendy Abdelsayed,
"Teta Habooba,"
who reposed in the Lord
on August 6, 2020.

Please remember us in your prayers
and help us hunger for righteousness
as you did.

FOREWORD

When I became Orthodox over a decade ago, I found myself in a spiritually difficult place. I was raised without any religious upbringing, and then after my many years in Protestant denominations, Orthodoxy Christianity's smoke and bells compelled me to see what was promised at the Eucharistic cup: Christ's healing presence, his body and blood mending the wounds I could only feel in my heart, my own life stretched over many losses and traumas. It was both the end and beginning of my pilgrimage, my entry into Orthodoxy. After receiving chrismation and Holy Communion, I realized that I had been the sparrow in Psalm 84, building a nest in Christ's doorway, only to see that I had been at his altar all along.

I had spent my Protestant years in faithful, loving church communities who lived out Micah 6:8's prophetic call: "Do justice, love mercy, and walk humbly with your God." I saw them involved in so many social ministries, ones that addressed the roots of social injustice with Christ's care and compassion. Yet I struggled to see this shared within my Orthodox communities, even as we proclaimed an unbroken line back to Christ. When my husband was in seminary at Holy Cross, the seminary for the Greek Orthodox Church of North America, I walked daily past the grave of Archbishop Iakovos, who famously marched with Martin Luther King. I read about St. Maria of Paris, who hid Jewish children in trash cans to save them from the Nazis. And as I wondered about their legacies, I also yearned for a voice in my own time to chronicle how Orthodox Christians addressed systemic social ills: poverty, injustice, care for the abandoned, and justice for the oppressed.

And then, I met Phoebe Farag Mikhail.

Phoebe and I connected in an online Orthodox women's group, where we found ourselves sharing a love for books, patristics, and words. We began a friendship that has spanned years of motherhood, clergy family life, and the many strains of this decade's political eruptions. And in those years, Phoebe's wisdom, righteousness, and generosity have sustained my faith and helped me see the wide history of Orthodox Christianity's devotion to biblical justice, particularly in her life as a Coptic Orthodox Christian. Her desire to share her tradition's own historical and theological practices, particularly in social ministries, has both inspired me and anchored me.

This devotional work, *Hunger for Righteousness,* has the power to help inspire and anchor all readers, regardless of their tradition. Rather than simply cataloguing Coptic Orthodox practices with an empty triumphalism, Phoebe has mapped a path through Lent that brings us to Christ where he said we would find him—in the poor, in prisons, in the sick and hungry and forgotten. It is a path that is open to all to follow—Orthodox, Catholic, and Protestant—and it is laid out for us with Phoebe's clear eye for beauty and theological acumen.

In our time, belligerence has become a virtue, and the voices of the loud and arrogant are too numerous to count. Phoebe's voice, however, brings us right to Christ, whose lifesaving love casts down our contemporary idols of power, violence, and empire. If we follow her words through Lent, I trust we will all see Christ as he has been: standing right beside us, lighting our paths in the darkness, his righteousness kindling courage in our hearts.

—Allison Backous Troy
Presbytera at St. Nicholas Greek Orthodox Church,
Grand Junction, Colorado

INTRODUCTION

One early spring many years ago in Queens, New York, my Catholic classmates in grade school asked me a confusing question: "What are you giving up this Lent?" I didn't understand. As a Coptic Orthodox Christian, I had much in common with my Catholic friends—we went to church on Sundays, took communion, went to confession, observed the major Christian holidays (although on different dates), and observed the Lenten season before Easter. We even each had our own pope. But as an Orthodox Christian, I never "decided" what I would give up for Lent.

In my church, we all "give up" the same things during Lent. We fast Lent as a community, and we call it Great Lent because it is the longest and most important one of many "lents" or fasts we practice all year. We don't have individual choices about what to "give up." In fact, we rarely use this word "give up" for any fasting period. In general, we fast the same way, abstaining from food until a certain time of day and then eating a vegan diet at other times. There are obviously allowances made for children, for pregnant and nursing women, and for those with medical conditions, but otherwise, no one decides what they will "give up" for Lent. Lent in Orthodoxy, like most things in Orthodoxy, is a corporate, communal endeavor, not an individual one. Yet even Orthodox Christians, especially those of us living in the West, have absorbed this highly individualized idea of Lent, narrowing its purpose to a period focused on personal spiritual piety.

Yet if we pay closer attention to the earliest Christian Lenten traditions, we'll discover how Lent was a period during which individuals who wanted to become Christian prepared themselves not for personal transformation, but to join the body of believers, the communion of saints, through baptism. By examining our liturgical prayers and Scripture readings developed over centuries, we'll discover the ways Lent has always been a time for individual repentance, yes, but first for giving and forgiving, for mending relationships and building new ones, for fighting injustice, and for growing in intimacy with God communally, not just individually.

The Coptic Orthodox Church of Alexandria's Lenten tradition has strong links to this early Christian heritage. Founded in the first century by St. Mark the Evangelist during his preaching in Alexandria, Egyptian Christianity spread and flourished throughout Egypt, becoming the primary religion of the country within a few centuries, despite brutal persecution by the Roman Empire. The months on the Coptic calendar date back to Egypt's Pharaonic period, but the Coptic Year begins in A.D. 284, during the reign of the Roman Emperor Diocletian, who brutally persecuted Christians, especially in Egypt. This book was published in the year 2025 Anno Domini, the year of our Lord, but also 1741 Anno Martyrum, the year of the martyrs. Egyptian Christianity survived through the centuries, even after the Arab invasion in the seventh century that eventually led to the conversion of many Egyptians to Islam, in part due to discrimination and sometimes persecution. During this period Egyptians became known as "Copts," an Arabization of the Greek word for "Egyptian." Eventually, only the Egyptian Christians were referred to as Copts. The Egyptian language, first written in hieroglyphs, then a Demotic script, and lastly in Greek letters with a few Demotic characters, became known as the Coptic language.

Outside of Church liturgical practice, most Egyptians have stopped speaking Coptic day to day, except as it survives in the unique vocabulary of Egyptian colloquial Arabic—and sometimes even in Modern Standard Arabic. The Arabic word for the Egyptian "crocodile," "timsa7" (تِمْساح) comes from the Coptic word for it: emsah (ⲙ̄ⲥⲁϩ). An Egyptian might ask you not to overthink something, and that word, "makmaka," comes from mokmek (ⲙⲟⲕⲙⲉⲕ) in Coptic, which means "to think" or "to ponder."[1] Some even believe the word "falafel," a favorite Lenten meal for Copts today, originated from a more modern Coptic phrase (Ⲫⲁ ⲗⲁ Ⲫⲉⲗ) that loosely translates to "of many beans," although this etymology is hotly debated.

Today Coptic Orthodox Christians are the largest population of Christians in the Middle East and North Africa, numbering

Introduction

between eight to ten million adherents, with almost one million more living outside of Egypt. Pope Tawadros is the 118th Patriarch of Alexandria, the See of St. Mark and All Africa in an unbroken line of apostolic succession that began with St. Mark before his martyrdom in Alexandria in A.D. 64. Although many of us in the West associate the title "Pope" with the Pope of Rome, church historian Eusebius records the earliest use of the title "Pope" in Christianity in reference to the thirteenth Alexandrian Patriarch, Pope Heracles. We continue to use this title for the patriarch of the Coptic Orthodox Church of Alexandria. We are a member of the Oriental Orthodox family of churches, along with our sister churches, the Armenian Orthodox Church, the Ethiopian Orthodox Tewahedo Church, the Eritrean Orthodox Church, the Indian Orthodox Church (Malankara Orthodox Syrian Church), and the Syrian Orthodox Church of Antioch. Each of these apostolic churches maintains a rich heritage of Orthodox Christianity that has been passed down from generation to generation.

While in this book I reference many different Christian church communions and traditions, I draw most upon the Coptic Orthodox tradition, since it's what I know best. Still, Lent is practiced globally by Christians from many denominations, because we all draw from the same well, and the well is deep and wide. I hope that readers unfamiliar with the Coptic Orthodox Lenten tradition find stories, practices, and perspectives that enrich their own traditions and discover how their church's Lenten practices align with the ones I share in this book. Most importantly, as we embark on this Lenten journey together, let us pray that together we might offer an acceptable fast to the Lord.

CHAPTER ONE

Where Does My Help Come From?

They told us it was just like walking up a wheelchair ramp. Well, two hours later, in pitch darkness, I lagged behind the rest of my group, wondering why this seemed easier for everyone else. Every step forward got harder and harder. I had not prepared well for this.

They told us that it was easier to climb Mount Sinai (Jabal Musa) in Egypt on foot than to take a camel. Climbers can take one of two paths: the "Steps of Repentance," a steep 3,750-step climb carved into the mountain by monks, and the "Camel's Path," a wide, winding slope that climbers share with camels. Both paths meet at a rest area before the final 750-step climb to the summit. I joined my church's group for the climb, excited to be walking where Moses had walked to meet with God and receive the Law. We took the Camel's Path and began at night so that we could see the sun rise at the top of the mountain and descend before the sun's heat battered the mountainside.

I struggled to make it to the final rest area before the last 750 steps. Inwardly ashamed, I stayed at the rest area with a few members of my group while the others journeyed to the summit. Most of those who stayed behind were much older than I and had knee problems, but one of them was a friend my age. As the rest of the group went up the stairs, she burst into tears. I turned to comfort her, thinking she was ashamed, like me, that she could not reach the top.

"I'm so happy," she said, between sobs. "This is my first time to ever climb a mountain! I did it!"

I swallowed my shame. In comparing my physical fitness to that of others, I had forgotten that this was my first climb, too. Even more importantly, I had almost forgotten that I was still sitting where Moses sat, where he might have even rested during his many days on this mountain. I thanked God for my friend's perspective. Turning with her, we watched the sun rise in silence. Unless we go back and try it again, we'll never know how it looked at the summit. But we know how it looked right there, and the sunrise still took my breath away.

I did not take up mountain climbing after that trip, and I have never gone back to Mount Sinai to try the climb again with more preparation. There are those who relish the hard work of mountain-climbing, the thrill of reaching the summit. I'm just not one of them. I prefer viewing mountains from afar, far enough to see their tops, and close enough to sense their majesty. I also enjoy seeing the view from a mountaintop, but not if I must climb for hours on foot in the middle of the night. While I know those mountaintop views are breathtaking, I'm not sure all the effort for that view is worth it. Thankfully, sunrises can be enjoyed at almost any altitude.

I much prefer walking to climbing. And in many ways, our spiritual lives can be likened to a walk. But along that walk sometimes there are hills, and sometimes mountains. And unlike the mountaintops we can reach by car, ski lift, or gondola, these spiritual mountains are the ones we must climb ourselves, like it or not.

Great Lent for me is one such mountain. Unlike physical mountains, Great Lent is a mountain I must climb as a Christian. I'll be honest—I often look towards the Great Lent climb with an impending sense of fatigue. I'd rather just skip to the Resurrection. I know this is a spiritual weakness on my part. Perhaps this is why the first book I wrote focused on the joy of the Resurrection, and the one spiritual practice I did not include was fasting.

The fact is, we do a lot of fasting, especially in Orthodox Christianity. All that fasting is for good reason. The church knows that most of us are not seasoned mountain climbers, and the church also knows that the safest mountain-climbing is done in groups. So, we fast together, with Lent arguably the most important fast of the year. Lent is a communal fast, a period when almost all Christians have decided to enter into a spiritual struggle. And, just as with climbing Mount Sinai in a group, we climb that spiritual mountain together.

Where Does My Help Come From?

Mountains hold a special place in Scripture—indeed, in all ancient Near Eastern religions. The idea of mountains as holy places seems ingrained in our human psyche. Mountains draw our eyes heavenward; their height, their majesty, their danger give us a glimpse of transcendence. Even as their summits seem out of reach, they paradoxically symbolize the nearness of God. "The elevation of mountains, as a geographical feature, qualified them to be a place of meeting between God the most high and His people on earth," Fr. Morcos Daoud writes.[2] Hence, Moses would receive the law on Mount Sinai, he would view the Promised Land on Mount Nebo, and the temple where the Israelites worshiped would be built on Mount Zion.

Our Lord Jesus Christ could often be found on a mountain. He went to a mountain to pray, to seek solitude from the crowds. He fasted and prayed for forty days and forty nights on the mountain where the devil tempted him. He met Moses and Elijah on Mount Tabor and was transfigured before his disciples. His most famous sermon is the Sermon on the Mount.

On that mountain, the Lord taught us what it means to be blessed. Matthew uses *makarios* for the word "blessed," and although, loosely translated, this word means "happy," its root goes much deeper. Orthodox author and peace activist Jim Forest writes that *makar* in classical Greek is related to the gods, to immortality. "In Christian use, *makarios* came increasingly to mean sharing in the life of God."[3] The poor in spirit, those who mourn, the pure in heart, the peacemakers, the meek, the merciful, those who hunger and thirst for righteousness—all who embody these qualities share in the life of God.

On that mountain, the Lord taught us how to share in the life of God by teaching us how to pray—how to communicate with God, how to be in relationship with him. The Lord told us to do some difficult things, like forgive those who have wronged us, love our enemies, turn the other cheek, and expect persecution. From a human perspective, these things are not just difficult, they can seem impossible. Without God, they *are* impossible.

Hunger for Righteousness

We might believe that like Moses, we will meet our Lord Jesus only if we make it to the top of the mountain, the heights of spirituality, the top of the ladder of divine ascent, and so on. The beauty of Lent, however, is that we don't need to wait until we reach the top. During Lent, Jesus climbs this mountain with us—just as he did in Matthew 5. He didn't fly to the mountain, despite having angels at his beck and call. He went up on the mountain with his own two feet.

During my first year of motherhood, I spent many hours alone at home with my firstborn. As much I treasured those days with him, I also often felt a crushing loneliness. I had just moved—twice. Once across the Atlantic to my parents' house, and once again into an apartment of our own. I was adjusting to new motherhood right as my husband was adjusting to his new role as a Coptic Orthodox priest.

Our apartment had a large balcony window, and from the sixteenth floor I had a view of the hills far beyond our street. Those hills became a comfort in my loneliness. Whenever I looked at them, Psalm 121 would come to my mind: "I will lift up my eyes to the hills—From whence comes my help? My help comes from the LORD, Who made heaven and earth." The hills stood far away, yet I could see them. Help from the Lord would come.

On that mountain in Matthew 5, Jesus said, "Blessed are those who hunger and thirst for righteousness, for they shall be filled." He did not say, "Blessed are those who *are* righteous." He said, Blessed are those who *hunger and thirst for it.* This is all he asks. He asks us only to *desire* righteousness, and he will fill us. He will fill us because Jesus Christ himself is righteousness, and all he asks is that we desire him. All we need to do is turn our eyes to the mountains. Our help will come from the Lord.

Books and books have been written on the Sermon on the Mount. In this book we will focus on this one Beatitude: "Blessed are those who hunger and thirst for righteousness, for they shall be filled." We'll explore in practical terms what it means to hunger and thirst for righteousness. We'll learn about righteous people and discover how their intimacy with God and love for their neighbors led to their being called righteous. And we'll use Great Lent as a chance to begin our ascent, our opportunity to cultivate a desire for that righteousness.

This book has ten chapters, this one being the first, so it is set up to be started before Great Lent begins and completed after the Feast of the Resurrection. For Coptic Orthodox, Ethiopian Orthodox, Eritrean Orthodox, and Syrian Orthodox Christians, this means that if you started this chapter the week of Jonah's Fast (the Fast of Nineveh), you can read one chapter per week, finishing the last chapter during the first week of the Holy Fifty Days. Eastern Orthodox readers can start with this chapter when the Lenten Triodion (the three-week period before the start of Great Lent) begins. Armenian Orthodox readers can start with this chapter during the Fast of the Catechumens, which for Malankara Indian Orthodox, Catholic, Anglican, and other Protestant readers also coincides with the three weeks before the start of Great Lent.

May we offer our Lord Jesus Christ an acceptable fast, during which our hunger and thirst for food and drink lead us to a hunger and thirst for righteousness. When we sing the refrain "Jesus Christ fasted for us/forty days and forty nights," we are not simply telling the story of what Christ did, but what he did for us and for our salvation. Through this fast he fasted for us, he was "paying in advance a deposit for our own fasting," St. Fr. Bishoy Kamel says, "so that when we fast, He is our partner in the journey of fasting. He set the plan, now He is our partner in it."[4] So, with the Lord himself as our partner on this climb, let us begin.

Part I
HUNGER AND THIRST

St. Abraam of Fayoum

Abba John the Dwarf said, 'A house is not built by beginning at the top and working down. You must begin with the foundations in order to reach the top.' They said to him, 'What does this saying mean?' He said, 'The foundation is our neighbour, whom we must win, and that is the place to begin. For all the commandments of Christ depend on this one.'

—Sayings of the Desert Fathers, 93[1]

Now what is hunger? Surely the desire for the food one needs. For when the physical vigour is gone, its lack is to be made up again by taking the necessary nourishment. Then nature desires bread, or something else to eat. If, therefore, someone took gold instead of bread into his mouth, would he meet the need? Hence, if a man cares for things he cannot eat instead of for food, he is evidently concerned with stones. While nature seeks one thing, he is busy trying to find another. Nature says—in fact, by being hungry it almost cries out—that it is now needing food. . . . But you do not listen to nature; you do not give it what it is seeking. You think instead of the load of silver you want to be on your table, and so you look for metalworkers. . . . Nature wants to drink—but you prepare costly . . . mixing bowls, jars, and a thousand other things which have nothing to do with the need in question. . . . This is the advice the enemy gives in the matter of food; such things he suggests by turning to stones, instead of being content with the ordinary use of bread. But He who overcomes temptation does not eliminate hunger from nature, as if that were a cause of evil. He only removes the worry and fuss which the counsel of the enemy causes to enter together with that need. He does not eliminate hunger, since it is needed to preserve our life; but He does sift out and cast away the superfluous things that have become mixed up with this need, when He says that he knows a bread that nourishes indeed, because the Word of God has adapted it to human nature. If, therefore, Jesus has been hungry, the hunger that is in us as it was in Him should truly be blessed. What is this food that Jesus is not ashamed to desire? . . . "My meat is to do the will of the Father." . . . Now if the Father desires that we should all be saved, and if, therefore, our life is Christ's food, we know how to make use of this hungry condition of the soul. What is this? That we should hunger for our own salvation, that we should thirst for the Divine Will, which is precisely that we should be saved.

—St. Gregory of Nyssa, Sermons on the Beatitudes[2]

CHAPTER TWO

TRAINING FOR THE CLIMB:
JONAH AND THE NINEVITES

Though I am not a mountain-climber, I imagine that anyone who sets out to climb a mountain needs ample preparation time, just like anyone who wants to run a marathon or compete in any physical sport. Showing up for a game without practice or starting a climb without preparation usually leads to failure at best, and injury or even death at worst. The most seasoned mountain climbers still must specially train for at least a year to be able to climb Mount Everest. Even then, people still die climbing that mountain. I don't recommend it.

Jumping into Lent without preparation can be as dangerous for us spiritually as trying to climb Mount Everest without preparation would be to us physically. Recognizing this need for preparation for the Lenten climb, many church liturgical calendars and lectionaries begin preparation for Great Lent well in advance of the fast. Catholics call the third Sunday before Lent Septuagesima, as it falls approximately seventy days before the Feast of the Resurrection. Anglicans, Lutherans, and others call the pre-Lent period "Shrovetide," and Eastern Orthodox churches call it the Lenten Triodion. In the Oriental Orthodox tradition the Nineveh Fast, or Jonah's Fast, precedes Great Lent by two weeks for the Copts, Ethiopians, and Eritreans, and by three weeks for the Armenians and Indians and Syrians.[1] In Appendix A, I provide a chart showing how these different terms align with each other on the liturgical calendar.

The Fast of Nineveh is a three-day fast that originated in the Syriac Orthodox Church and spread to the rest of the Oriental Orthodox Churches. It always starts on Monday, with the fast broken and the Passover of Jonah celebrated on Thursday. The Armenian Orthodox Church developed its own similar fast during the same week called the Fast of the Catechumens, a five-day fast with the fifth day in commemoration of the repentance of the Ninevites. In the Fast of Nineveh, believers fast a strict fast, which includes abstinence for a certain period of time, followed by eating only vegan foods, and for some ascetics, eating only bread and salt. Liturgies are prayed every day, often later in the afternoon.

Some churches prepare for Great Lent by easing into it, the way the Eastern Orthodox start by eating all their meat during Meatfare week (the second week of the Triodion), and then eating all their dairy during Cheesefare week (the third week of the Triodion). Jonah's Fast prepares us in a different way, by giving us a short foretaste of the coming Great Fast, the way sports teams play pre-season games before the official season, the way a student might take short, timed quizzes in preparation for a big test, or the way a new driver might drive for shorter distances for practice before taking a road trip. Even the hymns during Jonah's Fast in the Coptic Orthodox Church use the same tune as the hymns during Great Lent.

During Jonah's Fast we commemorate the city of Nineveh's three-day fast of repentance and the three days and nights that the prophet Jonah spent in the belly of the whale. The church recognizes these three days as a "type" or foreshadowing of the three days Christ would spend in the tomb before his resurrection from the dead. After the three days, we celebrate the Passover of Jonah and break the fast. Not only does it signal that it is time to prepare for Great Lent, but it is also a reminder of the Resurrection we will also celebrate when it is over.

The title of the biblical book of Jonah belies its contents, for although it is on the surface about the reluctant prophet Jonah, it is also about the repentance of Nineveh and above all, God's compassion and mercy. In it, God tells his prophet to go to Nineveh, an ancient Assyrian city located in what is now Mosul, Iraq, and preach that they will be destroyed because of their wickedness. Jonah refuses and takes a boat in the opposite direction so that he will not have to preach to the Ninevites. God then sends a storm that will not calm until the sailors fearfully throw Jonah overboard at his request.

Training for the Climb: Jonah and the Ninevites

Jonah then gets swallowed by a big fish that spits him up on the shore after three days. God tells him again to go to Nineveh, and this time he obeys. When he arrives at Nineveh and warns them of their impending doom, the Ninevites repent. Their king calls a fast, saying, "Who can tell if God will turn and relent, and turn away from His fierce anger, so that we may not perish?" (Jonah 3:9). After they spend three days and three nights fasting, God indeed turns from his anger and does not destroy them. Were Jonah's words, "Yet forty days, and Nineveh shall be overthrown," effective enough to spark the complete turnaround of the largest city of the Assyrian empire?

In his book *Contemplations on the Book of Jonah the Prophet*, His Holiness Pope Shenouda of blessed memory concludes that Nineveh's swift repentance had nothing to do with the effectiveness of Jonah's preaching. Rather, he believes it was due to the readiness of their hearts. "Their hearts were prepared for any word proceeding from the mouth of God. Thus their repentance was so powerful, for it sprang from within and not from without."[2] Something prepared the Ninevites from within, and it certainly wasn't Jonah.

Scripture doesn't tell us much about what prepared the Ninevites' hearts for Jonah's message. We know from the study of ancient history that Assyria fought ruthless military campaigns against its neighbors and enemies.[3] Perhaps the Ninevites, as a people, had tired of constant warfare. I would like to think it was Ashurbanipal's palace library in Nineveh, perhaps the first in the ancient world, but we don't know how many Ninevites had access to the palace library to prove this theory, and history places Jonah a good century before Ashurbanipal's reign. Could the Ninevites have heard about Jonah's prophecy to Jeroboam son of Joash? Jeroboam "restored the territory of Israel from the entrance of Hamath to the Sea of Arabah according to the word of the LORD God of Israel, which He had spoken through His servant Jonah the son of Amittai" (2 Kings 14:25). Perhaps Jonah's reputation preceded him.

What most likely happened is that God himself prepared their hearts. He gave Jonah the task of delivering his message, but only God can change hearts. Why did God need Jonah, then? Perhaps to honor his prophet, to link him forever to this great repentance story. Or, perhaps, the opposite—to humble him, to remind him that while he is God's messenger, God is still God.

More important for us is that we heed the "sign of the prophet Jonah" (Matthew 12:39) and ask God to prepare our own hearts, so that when we hear the call to repentance, we immediately turn to God. The story of the Ninevites is a story of hope for all of us. In his homily on repentance and almsgiving, St. John Chrysostom observed how the Ninevites were

> able to annul in three days such anger caused by sin. I want you to marvel at the philanthropy of God, who was satisfied with three days of repentance for so many transgressions. I do not want you to sink into despair, even though you have innumerable sins.[4]

If God can forgive more than 120,000 people's wickedness (Jonah 1:2), then surely he can forgive our sins, no matter how grave and how great in number. The Ninevites were Gentiles who could not "discern between their right hand and their left" (Jonah 4:11), yet knew enough of about God that when their king heard the prophecy he said, "Who can tell if God will turn and relent, and turn away from His fierce anger, so that we may not perish?" (3:9). If the ignorant Ninevites could trust in God's mercy and compassion, how much more can we trust in his mercy and compassion to forgive us of our sins?

In one Coptic Orthodox hymn we sing during the liturgies of both the Fast of Nineveh and Great Lent, we proclaim this trust confidently: "I know that You are good/compassionate and merciful/remember me with Your mercy/forever and ever."[5] In Coptic hymnology, important words in hymns are emphasized by lengthening the time spent singing that word. In this hymn, the word "know" goes on for ten seconds. I *know* God is good. I *know* he is compassionate. I *know* he is merciful. Trusting in this, I know it is time to prepare my heart for repentance and throw myself at God's goodness, compassion, and mercy.

Training for the Climb: Jonah and the Ninevites

Whether or not this was the original intent for it, the Fast of Nineveh prepares us for Lent practically as well. After three days of the strict vegan fast with abstinence, it makes us literally hungry for all the foods we could not eat—and giving us ten days to eat it before Great Lent begins. For the next ten days, barring those with health concerns, food allergies, eating disorders, those pregnant, nursing, or with other individual food-related concerns, we eat or distribute all the meat, fish, and dairy products in our homes to get ready for the fast ahead.[6] These days in the Coptic Orthodox Church are called "refaa3," literally meaning "lifting up" or "leave-taking."

Not every Christian tradition has continued the abstinence from meat, fish, and dairy in its practice of Great Lent. Nonetheless, it's important for all of us to recognize the main purpose of this form of abstinence: almsgiving. The Lenten diet was historically easier to follow for the financially poor because meat, fish, and dairy generally cost more money than grains, vegetables, fruits, and legumes. Those who could afford to eat meat and dairy on a more regular basis were supposed to give the cost of that food as alms. Those who abstained further by abstaining from food till a specific hour were to give the cost of the skipped meal or two to the poor as well.

In Leviticus 25, God commands that the people of Israel observe a "jubilee" every fifty years, to be announced with trumpets on, significantly, the Day of Atonement. During the fiftieth year, the Lord commanded the Israelites to "return every man unto his possession" (15:13, KJV). Regardless of how much land an Israelite purchased with his own wealth over the prior forty-nine years, during the Jubilee year that land would return to the family it originally belonged to, the portion they inherited from their forefathers. During the Jubilee year, "the earth kept the sabbath, debts were canceled, slaves were set free and, as it were, a new life was established again," writes St. Basil the Great.[7] The year of Jubilee would have happened once every generation and would be the great equalizer for the people of Israel, insuring that even those who were poor would not be poor forever, and that their children would not inherit their poverty but would inherit God's portion.

In many ways, the interconnectedness between the Lenten fast and almsgiving serves as an annual "jubilee" for Christians, a chance to take stock of all the excess that we have acquired and return some of it to those who do not have excess. And just as the pre-Lenten period is marked by a season of repentance, so too the Jubilee year was announced on the Day of Atonement (Yom Kippur)—the last day of a ten-day period of repentance, the holiest day on the Jewish calendar. Thus, the fruit of repentance then and now would not just be reconciliation between each individual and God, but restoration of the entire community to their inheritance from God.

Recently, I sat down and calculated how much my family of five spent on meat and dairy products in January and saw that they constituted about 50 percent of our total food budget for that month, even though they constituted a much lower percentage of our actual food by volume. If I am practicing Lenten almsgiving, I should now be giving a good portion of what I'm not spending on these items to those in need, as what is left is vegetables, fruits, grains, starches, and legumes, which are usually much less expensive than meat and dairy. Sometimes, this isn't always the case; there are some locations in North America, for example, where fresh produce is not always available. Some believers, for health reasons, might need to spend more money on more expensive vegan foods like avocados, nuts, and seeds. If Lent finds us spending the same amount or more on food to observe the fast, there might be other ways to incorporate almsgiving during Lent that are not related to money saved or spent.

For those who do save money during Lent, the pre-Lent period is a good time to decide where to donate the money saved from avoiding meat and dairy purchases and eating more simply. We can give to a local food pantry or soup kitchen, or a charity that works on hunger and food insecurity; or perhaps, if we know someone personally in need, we can drop a grocery gift card in their mailbox or do the grocery shopping for an elderly neighbor.

Whether or not we fast from meat and dairy, or whether or not we save money from this, knowing that almsgiving is the point means we can still find ways to offer to the physically hungry during the fast. Perhaps we can consider how many times a week or month we eat out, and we choose instead to eat at home and donate the cost of this meal to the hungry, or we deliver such a meal to someone who needs something hot and satisfying. Perhaps we can consider inviting others to our table during Lent. Hospitality is not just for feasting, and Lent is a beautiful time to make room in our hearts for others as we've made room in our pantries.

On that same trip to Egypt when we climbed Mount Sinai, our group visited a monastery in Wadi El-Natroun during mealtime, and the monks offered us a simple meal of rice with green peas and carrots. Unlike our other, more sumptuous meals at restaurants, at the monastery our Muslim bus driver sat with us at the same table. As we ate, I overheard him say, "the best meals I eat on these trips are at the monasteries." Elsewhere, he was the driver, relegated to eat a boxed meal on the bus while we dined in the restaurant. At the monastery, he was one of us. According to Isaiah, this is the fast that God has chosen:

> Is it not to share your bread with the hungry
> And that you bring to your house the poor who are cast out;
> When you see the naked, that you cover him,
> And not hide yourself from your own flesh? (58:6–7).

In choosing to abstain from certain foods for over a month and a half and giving what we would have fed ourselves to others, our almsgiving is less a charity than it is empathy and solidarity. In the words the Lord said to Isaiah, when we fast and give to the hungry and the poor, we are giving to our "own flesh" (58:7). When we experience what it is like to not eat or drink even when we are hungry or thirsty, we get a small taste of what it is like to live with water shortages, chronic hunger, food insecurity, and war. When we experience what it is like to limit the kinds of foods we eat, we get a small taste of what it is like to live with financial or health limitations that severely reduce our choices.

If we do experience war, chronic hunger, food insecurity, financial limitations, or health issues, Great Lent is for us, too. In first-century Rome, unwanted babies were left out in the elements to die of starvation, cold, or animal predators. Sometimes, they were taken and raised into the slave trade or sexual slavery. During this time, the early Christians rescued babies who had been "exposed" and raised them in the community. During worship these children, "who had nothing of their own to bring, always offered the water to be mingled with the wine in the chalice."[8] These children show us that if all we have to offer is some water, it is an acceptable offering. Mingled with the wine in the chalice, the water they offered became the blood of Christ.

If we do not have the financial means to give, we can consider ways to give of our other resources during Lent. Our time is often more valuable than money. We can offer that time to a food pantry, helping prepare hot meals or packing lunches. If we know how to assemble flat-packed furniture, we can help an elderly neighbor assemble a bookshelf. If we know of a harried mother of multiple young children who could use some time to breathe, we can offer to watch her children for a few hours. All of these offerings are precious gifts, a blessing to the body of Christ.

What we need to cultivate for Great Lent is not only a generosity of resources but also a generosity of spirit. Rachel Pieh Jones witnessed this kind of generosity firsthand during her time in Djibouti. In her book *Pillars: How Muslim Friends Made Me Closer to Jesus*, she describes how she once went with her friends Amina and Deeqa to understand how they made a living. Officially unemployed, these women carved out work for themselves by preparing hot breakfast, lunch, and tea to the construction workers working near the embassies and other wealthy neighborhoods. Struggling financially themselves, they bought most of their supplies from merchants on credit with the hopes that the workers paying for their meals that day would cover those debts, and that there would be enough left over for these women to feed their own families.

Jones watched Deeqa hand tea to men she knew could not pay, not bothering to write their names down in her credit notebook. She watched Amina note the men who were most hungry and save them the best pieces of bread. "Once I got to know Amina and Deeqa," Jones writes, "I stopped thinking of them as poor. . . . These women taught me about Djibouti's informal economy. They also taught me that giving doesn't have to come from wealth or abundance. All one needs is a generous heart."[9] When we consider our giving this Lent, let us consider it with a generous heart.

We might be the ones in need of alms. We may already know what it means to be truly physically hungry before a fast appeared on our calendar. Lent is our opportunity to consider what it means to have that hunger and thirst for righteousness, not just for food and drink. Lent is also our opportunity to receive love from our "own flesh," too, in the words of Isaiah. We might not have food to "lift up" during these weeks of preparation, but we can lift up others in prayer for our brothers and sisters. If we are the recipients of alms, we are also part of the circle of Lenten solidarity.

QUESTIONS FOR REFLECTION AND DISCUSSION:
1. Knowing how our churches help us prepare for Great Lent, how do we plan to prepare for the fast in our own lives?
2. In the Coptic Orthodox Church, a Lenten hymn sung during the distribution of the Divine Mysteries says, "Blessed are those who have mercy, Who give to the poor and fast and pray, The Holy Spirit will fill their hearts, The Son will show them mercy on judgement day." What does the order of these words say about role of giving during Lent?
3. What are the ways in which we plan to cultivate a generous heart during the upcoming fast? How will we give?

CHAPTER THREE

NEGOTIATING WITH GOD: ABRAHAM

Righteousness. We don't use this word very much in our culture, except perhaps in a derogatory way, when referring to someone as self-righteous—a person who judges others and believes they are holier than everyone around them, even if they are not. We love to hate self-righteous characters in movies and novels like Rachel Lynde in L. M. Montgomery's *Anne of Green Gables* or Mr. Collins in Jane Austen's *Pride and Prejudice*. We do, however, sympathize with characters who begin as self-righteous and then, by gaining humility, exhibit true righteousness, such as Peter in C. S. Lewis's *Chronicles of Narnia,* Mary in Laura Ingalls Wilder's *Little House* series, and, perhaps, the Jedi over the course of the Star Wars movies.

We rarely, however, use the word "righteousness." Yet, just as we know we need food and water when we are hungry and thirsty, we need to know exactly what we need when we are hungering and thirsting for righteousness. It isn't as concrete as food and water, so a dictionary definition won't be enough. What is righteousness? What does it mean? How does it look? In the over 600 times the word appears in the Bible, who do the Scriptures call righteous?

Although Abel and Noah are called righteous in Genesis, the first character in the Bible called righteous that we get to know more fully is Abraham. Of Abraham, Genesis 15:6 says, "And he believed in the LORD, and He accounted it to him for righteousness." This verse is quoted again several times in the New Testament in Romans, Galatians, and James. Clearly, the authors of Scripture see Abraham's righteousness as particularly significant and worth examining.

In the Genesis account, we meet Abram at age 75, when God tells him to leave Haran, where his father, Terah, had settled, with the promise to make him the father of many nations. We don't know anything about him at this point, other than that his wife, Sarai, has not had any children. Without discussion, Abram, his wife, his nephew Lot, Lot's wife and children, the "people they had acquired in Haran," whom we can assume were slaves, all go to Canaan. Abram believes God's promise and leaves Haran before ever seeing the promise fulfilled.

On this verse, St. Augustine compares Abram's great faith in God to our weak faith as Christians: "He had received nothing from [God] and he believed his promise. We do not yet believe him, though we have already received so much."[1] We have received Scripture that recounts God's faithfulness in his promises. Abram had no Scripture to read and repeat to himself or his children. We have Christ's incarnation, death, and resurrection to demonstrate God's love for us. Abram lived thousands of years before the Incarnation. We have experienced baptism and communion with the body of believers. Abram experienced none of this, and yet he believed.

Abram and his entourage go to Canaan, a land that encompasses what is now Israel, the West Bank, Gaza, Jordan, and parts of Syria and Lebanon. Though the Lord promises this land to Abram and his descendants, Abram doesn't actually settle where the Canaanites live. After building an altar to the Lord there he moves on, building another altar where he pitches his tent, with Bethel to the east and Ai to the west. The ancient cities of Bethel and Ai are considered today to be in the modern-day West Bank. He then travels to the Negev, a desert area in the southern part of modern-day Israel, and when he finds a famine there, he continues south towards Egypt to avoid this famine.

A curious turn of events happens while Abram passes through Egypt. We'll look more closely at this part of the story in a later chapter. For now, it's important to note that Abram leaves Egypt with great riches given to him by the Egyptians. If you've ever been to a museum displaying ancient Egyptian antiquities, it's not hard to imagine the level of wealth the Egyptians had to share, and Abram receives a good portion. If we continue following Abram's path, we find him in Genesis 13, Abram going "up from Egypt" with his wife, all his possessions, and his nephew Lot, and returning to the place between Bethel and Ai, where he pitches his tent and makes an altar to the Lord.

Negotiating with God: Abraham

The Canaanites and the Perizzites also live in this area, but Abram has no conflicts with them. Rather, the conflicts happen between Abram's and Lot's herdsmen. The land they have chosen to settle on is not enough to sustain both Abram's and Lot's possessions. Literally, "Now the land was not able to support them, that they might dwell together, for their possessions were so great" (13:6).

Note here that the reason for their inability to dwell together is not that they personally don't get along; the source of their strife is their great possessions. They both own too much; there is no room for all their possessions in one place. Only one path seems clear to Abram for the two families to live without strife: they must separate, each choosing a different land to dwell on. Abram does not want strife between them, because they are brethren.

Interestingly, neither Abram nor Lot consider a different path—a path, perhaps, on which they might rid themselves of some of their possessions in order to live peacefully together in the same place. St. Ambrose blames Lot for their inability to do so, inferring that Lot was the source of the problem:

> [I]ndeed, no space can be large enough for those who love discord.
> . . . Even limited spaces are more than adequate for those who are
> meek and peace-loving, while for those whose mentality is one of
> discord even wide open spaces are too restricted.[2]

St. Ambrose here echoes the words of Proverbs: "Better is a dinner of herbs where love is, Than a fatted calf with hatred" (15:17). Nonetheless, neither Abram nor Lot considers the possibility of reducing their possessions. However, we do see Abram put Lot before him, asking Lot to choose the land he would like to live on, with Lot taking the more attractive-looking land, and Abram taking the second choice.

As I write this chapter, war rages in the Gaza Strip between modern-day Israel and Hamas, with a grievous death toll of thousands of innocent civilians, and no chance for lasting peace in sight. Almost everyone involved in that battle, whether fighter, victim, supporter, or bystander, considers this same Abram their forefather. I wonder how heartbroken Abraham must be right now, looking down at his many descendants, greater than the stars in the sky, and unable to live in peace with each other, unable to put their cousins before themselves the way Abram did for Lot. We call ourselves children of Abraham, but we don't behave as he did, finding a solution to the strife so that brethren could dwell peacefully, favoring others above himself.

It is after this moment, after Abram asks Lot to choose where he would live, and after Lot separates himself from Abram, that God tells Abram, "Lift up now your eyes, and look from the place where you are—northward, and southward, eastward, and westward: For all the land which you see I give to you and to your descendants forever" (Genesis 13:14–15). The first time God makes this promise to Abram is when Abram gives Lot the better land. In the words of St. John Chrysostom, it is as if God were saying to Abram,

> You . . . gave evidence of your eminent humility and showed
> such concern for peace as to put up with anything for the sake of
> preventing any rivalry coming between you—accept from me a
> generous reward.[3]

Abram here does not hunger and thirst for the best land, or for domination over his relative. He hungers instead for restraint, humility, and peace, and God satisfies him with the promise that all the land will be his, and that He will make his descendants "as the dust of the earth: so that if a man could number the dust of the earth, then your descendants also could be numbered" (Genesis 13:16).

However, God doesn't satisfy Abram with the land right away, nor with the descendants right away. God satisfies Abram with a promise. And Abram believed God. Before receiving his reward, he believed God would give it to him. This faith in God's promise was credited to him as righteousness. But why would Abraham believe God would provide this abundant promise, when God had not yet even provided him with a child?

The answer Genesis offers us is not Abraham experiencing God's power or receiving God's gifts, but Abraham experiencing God's *friendship* and receiving God's love. This friendship flourishes throughout Abraham's life. When he goes to rescue Lot from captivity (14:12) and refuses to loot the captors or to receive gifts from the King of Sodom (14:23) but rather gives King Melchizedek a tithe and receives bread and wine (14:18–20), God tells Abram that he is Abram's "exceedingly great reward"—the alternative translation being "your reward will be very great" (15:1).

In modern society we have, in many ways, lost our understanding of friendship and how essential it is for human flourishing. In his book *Jesus, the Great Philosopher*, Jonathan Pennington describes the way our culture has "become so eroticized" that we struggle to enjoy and invest in friendships without the suspicion (or expectation) of sexual attraction, whether between men and women or between people of the same gender.[4]

Consider the television sitcom *Friends*, popular in the late 1990s and early 2000s. Four out of the six "friends" on the sitcom have a sexual relationship with another one of the "friends" at some point in the series, making it less a show about friendship than about the inevitability of sexual attraction between men and women who spend enough time together. The medical drama *Grey's Anatomy* would make us believe that even medical colleagues of any gender cannot possibly work together for long hours without sexual attraction.

Abraham's intimate friendship with God elevates the meaning of friendship for all of us. Friendship, pursued rightly, can nourish us and grow us into better people. The best friendships are not the ones that close us in—like cliques—but orient us outwards, towards welcoming others, towards helping others. My dearest and most life-affirming friends are the ones with whom I have created, served, volunteered, pilgrimed, and done mission work. Friendship can help us sustain our other important relationships—with our spouses and other family members—precisely by unburdening those relationships of the expectation of the emotional support and companionship that only friendship can provide. Many marriages in fact dissolve because of the unrealistic expectation that spouses should meet all of our emotional and relational needs. They simply cannot. That's what friends are for.

The church has recognized and blessed the sacred nature of friendships. As long ago as the fourth century in Egypt, the church had a ritual ceremony called "brother making" that cemented spiritual friendships. This ceremony made adoptive brothers and sisters out of friends who were on a lifelong spiritual journey together. In Egypt, this was done with monks. In 1985, two scholars of Syriac Christianity, Susan Ashbrook Harvey and Robin Darling Young, decided to visit the Syriac East together, spending three weeks visiting the ancient holy sites that they had studied for decades in academia. During the final portion of their pilgrimage, they visited the Church of the Holy Sepulchre in Jerusalem and met the Syriac Archbishop, who saw their unique bond and asked them to join him for an ancient ritual after the Divine Liturgy (known as "Mass" in the Catholic Church). After the liturgy, while still fully vested, Archbishop Mar Dionysius Behnam Jajaweh led Ashbrook Harvey and Darling Young to the tomb of Christ, where he wrapped his liturgical garment on both of their right hands and prayed an ancient prayer in Syriac. "And then he announced to us that we were now sisters forever. And so it was," says Darling Young.[5] This sisterhood was built on their shared research interests in ancient Syriac Christianity and the connection they had woven during their pilgrimage through these sacred sites. After their trip they each returned to their own homes and institutions (Ashbrook Harvey to Rhode Island and Darling Young to Washington, DC), still connected at a distance through this ancient ritual.

If sacred friendships like these can bring us closer to God, imagine a friendship with God, like Abram's. Still, Abram is human, like the rest of us. When God tells him that he himself is Abram's reward—or that his reward will be very great, which is the translation many of the Fathers base their commentary on—Abram wonders—wonders!—what God has to offer him, since he has no heir. God, ever faithful despite Abram's failings, reminds Abram of his promise, not just of descendants but of the land. Abram believes God, though it will still be years before he will see the promises come to fruition. Even when Abram and Sarai take matters into their own hands and bear Ishmael through Hagar, God blesses Hagar and Ishmael too, while remaining faithful to his promise and giving Abram the promised Isaac many years later.

Negotiating with God: Abraham

God changes their names, too, from Abram to Abraham, and from Sarai to Sarah, signifying an even deeper relationship, a transformative one. Abraham recognizes the Lord when he welcomes the three strange visitors at the oak of Mamre and serves them. Abraham shows love and hospitality not just for his neighbor, but for the stranger, running to welcome them and hurrying to offer them refreshment.

The intimacy of this friendship is such that Abraham is actually able to negotiate with God. In Genesis 18, God warns Abraham that he intends to destroy Sodom and Gomorrah. Abraham answers God and says, "Would You also destroy the righteous with the wicked? Suppose there were fifty righteous within the city; would You also destroy the place and not spare it for the fifty righteous that were in it?" (23–24). So God answers Abraham and says, "If I find in Sodom fifty righteous within the city, then I will spare all the place for their sakes" (26). But Abraham doesn't stop there. He continues to negotiate. "Suppose there were five less than the fifty righteous," Abraham says. "would You destroy all of the city for lack of five?" (27). Astoundingly, God agrees.

Abraham doesn't stop. He keeps negotiating. "Since he saw God was predisposed to kindness," as St. John Chrysostom says, suppose there are forty righteous? God agrees. Suppose there are 30? God agrees. Suppose there are 20? God agrees. Suppose there are 10? God agrees. I want to know how I can be so intimate with God that I can negotiate with him the way Abraham did. How many of us would love to be so close to God in this way that our words can go so far as to possibly influence God?

Our Lord Jesus Christ tells us that we are blessed if we hunger and thirst for righteousness—if we desire this intimacy with God that the righteous Abraham had. We don't need to actually have this intimacy yet. All we must do is want it, badly. Hunger for it. Thirst for it. We don't even need perfection to have this righteousness, either. Scripture calls Abraham righteous, but it does not describe him as perfect. Yet he is still called righteous, righteous enough to meet with God face-to-face and have discussions with the Almighty. Righteous enough that the Pantocrator told Abraham his plans, and Abraham negotiated with him about them.

Let's return to that astounding passage. Indeed, Abraham negotiates with God, but *what* he negotiates with him is the salvation of an evil city. He negotiates not for more land, or for offspring for himself, but for the saving of a city for the sake of a few righteous people in it. The heart of Abraham's intimacy with God consists of love for others—love, in fact, for a people he does not even know.

Indeed, our examination of Abraham's life here shows his care for others above himself. He gives Lot the choice of land. He does not take spoils from Sodom when he saves Lot from captivity. He offers a tithe to Melchizedek. He runs to serve the three strangers who come to his tent. His intimate friendship with God reflects outward, towards others. The closer Abraham becomes to God, the more he becomes like God.

Let's compare Abraham to our friend Jonah, who we talked about in the previous chapter. While Abraham is called righteous by Scripture, Jonah is not. Christ calls him a prophet, and 2 Kings 14:25 also calls him a servant of God, but nowhere does Jonah get described as righteous. We might, in fact, consider him the opposite of righteous, if we compare him to Abraham. When God told Abraham to leave his father's home and go to an unknown place, Abraham went. When God told Jonah to go to Nineveh, Jonah went, too—in the opposite direction.

Abraham brought blessing when he followed God's direction. Jonah almost sank a ship when he went in the opposite direction. While both Abraham and Jonah seemed to have direct access to God, their conversations with God went very differently. Jonah prayed to God in the belly of the fish for deliverance. Jonah complained to God when Nineveh was *not* destroyed. Jonah complained to God when the plant that gave him shade was withered. Jonah's conversations with God were about himself. Only God demonstrated concern for others in these conversations, not Jonah.

In stark contrast, Abraham's remarkable negotiation with God, the back and forth that we see repeated again with Moses negotiating on behalf of the Israelites, reflects a faith in God for who he really is. Interestingly, Jonah himself acknowledges this when he complains that God has *not* destroyed Nineveh. "I knew you would be compassionate and not destroy them!" He says to God, angrily. Jonah wanted fire to come down from heaven on Nineveh as it did for Sodom. But Sodom did not repent—Nineveh did.

It is the Ninevites, not Jonah, who negotiate with God. They are not so near to God that they might have a discussion, like Abraham, but somehow, they intuit that perhaps God might relent due to their fasting, prayer, and repentance. Abraham's intimacy with God was refined through long periods of trust and walking with him. The Ninevites give us hope that even those of us who are not as near to God as Abraham have our path to him through fasting, prayer, and repentance. As with Abraham's negotiation, fasting, prayer, and repentance change God's mind.

St. John Chrysostom points out that the Ninevites were "unacquainted with the method of the lovingkindness of God," and "had no other Ninevites to look to, who had repented and been saved. They had not read the prophets or heard the patriarchs, or benefited by counsel, or partaken of instruction . . . and yet they repented with all carefulness." The Ninevites give us comfort, in St. John Chrysostom's eyes.

> Was Nineveh destroyed? Quite the contrary. It arose and became more glorious, and all this intervening time has not effaced its glory. And we all yet celebrate it and marvel at it, that subsequently it has become a most safe harbor to all who sin, not allowing them to sink into despair but calling all to repentance, both by what it did and by what it gained from the providence of God, persuading us never to despair of our salvation.[6]

Thus while we hunger and thirst for the righteousness of Abraham that made him so much an intimate friend of God, so intimate that he would negotiate for the salvation of an evil city, so the church gives us the upcoming season of Lent to remind us that the tools are there for us to negotiate our own salvation, too. We might not have Abraham's righteousness just yet, but we have fasting, prayer, and repentance. If Abraham is our intercessor, the Ninevites are our "safe harbor." Somehow, whether we are Abraham or Nineveh, God is for us a shield, our exceedingly great reward.

Hunger for Righteousness

QUESTIONS FOR REFLECTION AND ACTION:

1. Moses is also called righteous in Scripture. How might we compare Moses to Abraham?
2. What does Jonah's story teach us about serving God?
3. How can our friendships help us hunger for righteousness?

CHAPTER FOUR

FRIEND OF THE POOR: ST. ABRAAM OF FAYOUM

Many Christians behave more like Jonah than Abraham in our prayers. We want our compassionate, loving, and merciful God, but we want him for ourselves. We want Him to be loving and forgiving to us, only. We don't concern ourselves with those different from us, with those outside our communities. We have even less interest for this love towards our enemies. Those Christians who do demonstrate love for everyone without distinction seem abstract, radical, perhaps. It's easy to dismiss them, to admire them from afar, and to think to ourselves, "I can never be this way."

This was my struggle with St. Abraam of Fayoum—friend of the poor, a radical giver, and a strict ascetic. His life, like that of Abraham, his namesake, is the definition of righteousness. Yet, sometimes, reading about him and discovering how radical and ascetic he was makes me a little uncomfortable.

Born in 1829 to pious Christian parents in a village in the southern Egyptian governorate of Mallawi, Bulus (Paul) Ghobrial lost his mother at the age of eight. He received his education at a church school, where he demonstrated a love for hymns and other religious subjects. This led to his ordination to the diaconate at age 15, and by age 19 he had taken monastic vows and joined the Monastery of St. Mary (El-Muharraq) in Assiut. This monastery is famous for being the location of the resting place of the Holy Family for six months during their flight to Egypt. There he was ordained a priest, and his fellow monks loved him, electing him head of the monastery when its former abbot died.

As head of the monastery, Fr. Bulus developed its agricultural lands and increased its income, while also making it a haven for the poor people of the community, who numbered in the thousands, and to whom he gave of the monastery resources indiscriminately.[1] Although he had also enriched the monastery by developing its agricultural lands, Fr. Bulus's fellow monks did not like seeing all the monastery's income spent in this way, and they appealed to the area bishop to remove him. From there, Fr. Bulus went to the Monastery of St. Mary (El-Baramus) in Wadi El-Natroun, where he continued to give whatever he had to anyone in need, including the Arab Bedouins who roamed the desert in the area near his cell. The abbot of this monastery eventually became Pope Cyril V, and he ordained Fr. Bulus bishop of the diocese of Fayoum.

As Bishop Abraam, he continued his practice of giving indiscriminately to the poor, to both Christians and Muslims. He often ate his own meals with them and tolerated no discrimination between rich and poor, a radical posture in Egypt's classist culture, exacerbated under British colonial rule.[2] A famous Arabic movie about his life portrays Bishop Abraam confronting his cook after hearing numerous complaints of the cook's contemptuous treatment of the poor. The cook swears "on his own eyes" that he does not discriminate between the rich and the poor. Later, however, the bishop catches him in the act of carelessly throwing plates to the poor eating at the table and yelling at them when they complain about the cold food with very little meat. He asks the cook if he served the same meat to the wealthy visitors who came to eat just a few hours before, and the cook admits that he gave the wealthy visitors much better food.

Bishop Abraam reprimands the cook for his treatment of the "brethren of Jesus" and dismisses the cook, who is still indignant and unrepentant. A few scenes later, the former cook comes to the Bishop weeping because his eyes have gone blind. Bishop Abraam prays for him, asking God to lift this punishment from him if his repentance is sincere. Not only did St. Abraam want his cook to treat the rich and the poor equally, but he also wanted him to be honest with himself.

St. Abraam's asceticism and giving went hand in hand. He did not allow himself any luxury that he did not give to others. He kept no money and no extra clothes or furniture. Any extra shawl or cloth given to him, he gave right away to someone in need of it, or in need of the money they could get by selling it. He did the same with furniture, giving it away to anyone who had need of it, while he himself lived in squalor.

The British travel writer S. H. Leeder's third book about Egypt, *Modern Sons of the Pharaohs: A Study of the Manners and Customs of the Copts of Egypt,* published in 1918, recounts his learning of Bishop Abraam's reputation for holiness and Leeder's great longing to meet him. In his account he described how his elite Egyptian guides in Fayoum were hesitant to take the visiting Englishman to Bishop Abraam's living quarters, which were attached to the church. Leeder remarks that these Copts have seen the luxurious headquarters of the British Archbishop in England and want Leeder to meet their bishop in the same sort of environment. I wonder if they thought an outsider might laugh or be disgusted by this holy man and the dire poverty in which he intentionally lived. I wonder if they themselves were disgusted.

Yet Leeder persisted in wanting to meet Bishop Abraam. His next problem, though, was that the bishop himself refused to see Leeder—unless the "distinguished Englishman" had a need. Bishop Abraam had no interest in being admired or gawked at. This visitor from the colonizing country could come to him only if he needed a blessing. In Leeder's words,

> The old man apparently had no liking for the idea of being sought out by travelers as a celebrity; this was not his Master's work. If the Englishman was poor, or sad, or ill, or had need in any way of spiritual ministration, or counsel, then he would see him, but not otherwise.[3]

At this time in Egypt, the British colonizers were equally disliked by most ordinary Muslim and Christian Egyptians. Leeder wrote in the preface of his third book, "Egypt and its native people . . . have become the centre of new interest through a realisation of its vital importance to the very existence of our empire." Leeder himself belonged squarely to the colonists and their colonial mentality.

As did the Ottoman and French colonizers before them, the British used "divide and conquer" tactics to maintain control over the Egyptian population. In governance, they gave the most important roles to non-Egyptian Christians, such as Syrians and Armenians, as well as Western Protestant missionaries coming from Europe and the United States. This served to perpetuate ill will among the larger Muslim population towards Christians in general, while still excluding the indigenous Christian population from most positions of authority.

The British also facilitated the establishment of missions from other Christian denominations that looked down on the Copts. Finding it difficult to evangelize the non-Christians in Egypt, these missionaries turned their sights on Coptic Orthodox faithful, whose sacramental and liturgical forms of worship were foreign to the foreigners. With only a few exceptions, most of the missionaries chose not to learn from the local Christian community or offer support to strengthen it. Rather, many tried to mold it into the form of Christianity they knew. Internally, the Coptic Orthodox Church itself was undergoing its own challenges, including conflict between the Patriarch and the lay council ("Magliss el Milli") over financial control of church assets.[4]

In this precarious situation emerged Bishop Abraam. St. Abraam stood in stark contrast to both the colonizers and the church leadership as someone who never fought for resources. He simply gave them all away. And he was just as generous with his blessings and prayers as he was with his finances. Leeder notes that there as "as many Moslems as Christians" making long pilgrimages to meet him. "There is no difference in the eager faith they all show in his power to help them in all their sorrows and difficulties."[5] This attitude is notable at a time when a radical Islamist group was also forming in Egypt that would wreak great havoc on Egyptian society—the Muslim Brotherhood. Righteousness attracts everyone.

Leeder eventually gets to meet St. Abraam by remembering that he has indeed been ill due to his "weak throat" a few years prior and can thus truthfully say that he has need of prayers for his health. When he arrives at the bishop's residence, Leeder describes the floor of the room outside the bishop's quarters as "black with grime," with windows "opaque with dirt." When he enters the bishop's room, he notes it is in a similar state—until he meets the bishop himself:

Friend of the Poor: St. Abraam of Fayoum

It was with deep emotion that I looked into the face of this modern saint. To doubt his right to the title was impossible, for the power of a pure and beautiful soul made itself felt at once, with a force that was almost overwhelming.[6]

At his encounter with St. Abraam, Leeder's condescending tone towards Egyptians recedes. St. Abraam has humbled him. When Leeder asks for a blessing for himself and his wife, St. Abraam holds his cross over their heads and begins praying in Coptic, and although Leeder only understands the words *Kyrie Eleison*, he says, "never had I heard prayer which seemed to establish a link with the Throne of Grace with such instant security; it seemed as if earth fell away, to leave this man speaking in the clear presence of God Himself."[7] St. Abraam transfigured the dreary room. Instead of uncleanliness, he emanated purity. Instead of clear windows, he himself was a transparent window into heaven.

On the beatitude "blessed are those who hunger and thirst for righteousness," theologian William Barclay explains that being righteous has two sides to it: both right living and right giving. He gives the example of those who live uprightly and morally, yet are "cold and hard and without sympathy . . . They are good, but they are cold." At the same time, there are those who sometimes behave immorally, drink excessively, and speak with profanities, but "if anyone else is in trouble, they would . . . give him their last penny without a thought of grudging it. Their morals may be erratic, but their heart is warm." Neither of these is righteous; rather each only has a part of righteousness. The "hunger and thirst" for righteousness is a hunger and thirst for the whole of righteousness. The grammatical case in the New Testament Greek words for "hunger" and "thirst" in the verse imbues the words with this meaning—hunger and thirst not for a part of something, but for the entirety of something; not just for a piece of bread, but for a whole loaf of bread. "The Christian goodness," Barclay writes, "is a complete goodness in which virtue and love join hands."[8] He then asks us the hard question: knowing righteousness is both of these, do we really want it? Do we really hunger and thirst for the whole of righteousness?

St. Abraam embodied "virtue and love" joining hands throughout his life, in the whole of his life. Yet, when I consider St. Abraam, I have to be honest. I don't know if I really want the radical lifestyle he had. I don't know how I could achieve both his extreme asceticism and his all-encompassing, radical love. I'm not sure how appropriate it is for me to imitate him exactly. After all, he was a celibate bishop in Egypt a century ago, and I am a married mother in the New York Metropolitan suburbs.

Still, he challenges me. Just when I think my house is too small, my pantry a little boring, or my wardrobe lacking interest, I read St. Abraam's story or come across a picture of him and realize how much more space I have than many others do, how I could have less to eat, how I could give away half of my closet and still have more than enough to wear. I can live on much less than I do, and I should. And yet, the space I have is being used by my family, and it's also where we are learning how to live together in virtue and in love. The extra food in my pantry makes spontaneous hospitality much easier.

Tish Harrison Warren writes about a balance between stable and radical in her book *Liturgy of the Ordinary*. Her friend Steven, who rents her garage apartment, is a little bit like St. Abraam. He spends his days in their city working with the homeless, growing vegetables in a community garden with them to both feed the homeless and build community with them. Warren writes,

> Steven's days look really different from mine. I hear him come and go throughout the day, on his way to do good in the world while I sit at my writing desk or change a diaper or sweep up crackers that my toddler threw on the floor. It's easy for me to think that Steven is doing the real work of God, that he is the peacemaker, that his life and work count and give God pleasure, while I'm sidelined.[9]

Contemplating St. Abraam makes me feel sidelined like this, too. However, it might be that we need the radicals like St. Abraam, like Steven, to show us that such a life is possible, to edge us towards discomfort, to examine ourselves and ask if we truly can give more, do more, love more. "We need [Steven]," Warren writes, "to be the prophet he is, to never let us forget that the poor are among us. We need him to constantly expand our horizons beyond our front door."[10]

Yet Warren also points out that Steven needs her and she needs him. Steven said to her once, "You and Jonathan [her husband] stabilize me. And I hope to destabilize you." Steven finds rest and comfort in Warren's day-to-day family life, while he also embodies the daily reminder to them of the poor and marginalized people who crave this same rest and comfort.

There's a small icon that rests above the door of St. Abraam's shrine in Egypt. It has been copied and displayed all over the shrine compound many times over. It shows St. Abraam with two people on either side of him and his two hands held open: on one side, his hand opens to receive alms from the wealthy person, who is standing; on the other side, his hand opens to give alms to the poor person, who is kneeling. The hand giving to the poor person is aflame. This flame could refer to a story told of St. Abraam putting his cross on the head of a demon-possessed man, causing the demon to cry out, "The fire! The fire!," and leave the man he was possessing.[11] Or, it could reference and interpret a famous saying of the Desert Fathers:

> Abba Lot went to see Abba Joseph and said to him, 'Abba, as far as I can I say my little office, I fast a little, I pray and meditate, I live in peace and as far as I can, I purify my thoughts. What else can I do?' Then the old man stood up and stretched his hands towards heaven. His fingers became like ten lamps of fire and he said to him, 'If you will, you can become all flame.'[12]

Indeed, in the Christian life, what is left after praying, fasting, meditating, purifying our thoughts, and keeping peace with others? In the words of Christ, it is to love our neighbors as ourselves. Perhaps Abba Joseph means that becoming "all flame" is that true, indiscriminate love for our neighbors that St. Abraam demonstrated in his life.

Contemplating on that icon made me realize that this is the most complete icon of St. Abraam. All three persons in the icon represent him—he is the rich person, both financially because of all that is given to him and spiritually because of his relationship with God; in both cases, he is always giving. And at the same time, he is poor, always willing to receive because the need is great, never accumulating for himself, so he can live like the poor.

We could also look at this icon in a different way. Behind each person in the icon is a dome of a church with a cross above, in the traditional Coptic style. We could consider this an icon of the Church and ask ourselves where we might stand in it. Sometimes, we might be the giver on one side. At other times, we are the receiver on the other side. And sometimes, we are both, like St. Abraam. It says to us that all those postures are holy, all are saintly, if centered on Christ. Freely receive, freely give.

The hunger for righteousness starts with wanting to be somewhere in the icon, even if we don't already see ourselves in it. If we do see ourselves somewhere, let's lean into that. If we are in the place of giving, let us give with more humility and love. If are in the place of receiving, let us accept with grace and humility. I thirst for this ability to be both, like St. Abraam. To be able to part with what has been given to me before it even registers as a possession; to be able to receive with a humble heart, and to be completely aflame the entire time because of Christ dwelling in me.

We began this section by recognizing ourselves in Jonah's resistance to God's love and forgiveness towards his enemies, the Ninevites. At the end of the book of Jonah, when Jonah sits angrily watching Nineveh not burn, God asks him, "Do you well to be angry?" Then, he teaches Jonah a lesson, giving him a plant to seek shade under, then destroying the plant. God tells Jonah that if he could care so much for just one plant that he did nothing to grow, how much more would he, an infinite God, care for a great city full of people who bear his image? God is not satisfied only with the repentance of Nineveh, nor is he satisfied with Jonah's obedience. He wants more from Jonah. He wants Jonah to love as he loves. He wants for Jonah that complete righteousness, that "virtue and love" joining hands, so that he can be blessed.

We don't see Jonah hungering for this righteousness, at least not in the biblical story. And so we also don't see him blessed or satisfied. What God wants for Jonah, he wants for us, too. He wants us to love even those we have been taught to despise. He wants us to give willingly and freely like St. Abraam, not angrily and by force, like Jonah. He wants us to be blessed, to be happy, to be filled.

Friend of the Poor: St. Abraam of Fayoum

1. Who are the saints who make us feel uncomfortable? What is it about their lives that make us feel uncomfortable, and how can we understand them better in order to learn from them?

2. Where do we see ourselves in the icon of St. Abraam? How can we grow in this?

3. How many of us have prayed honestly and earnestly for those with whom we disagree politically and ideologically? How would prayer change our perspective on those we disagree with?

Part II
RIGHTEOUSNESS

St. Paësia and St. John the Little

Often you have caused their (the poor people's) heart to be distant from God because you do not give them a break and your labors are so many, and you have caused them to sleep with groans, and their tears have mixed with their prayers because of your acts of abuse. Your concerns have become the meditations of the wretched ones day and night, instead of Psalms, thanks to the abundance of the anger of your wrath. Many slaves and lots of timid poor people have feared you more than the God who made them because of the burden that your numerous tasks impose upon them, just like those of Pharaoh of old, and they have given up their fasts. They have been more worried about getting to the doors of your house punctually than about getting to the church. On top of all this, you ignore them, cast them away from your door, and neither answer them nor show mercy to them. They have waited upon your words so that they might do them quickly, rather than upon the commandments of salvation that God has commanded them. They have learned from you to bear up as they attend you – and you do not allow them to kneel or sit down – rather than to stand before God to beseech him to prepare for them salvation from their poverty and also to forgive them the sins of their ignorance. The thought of the interest payments that you double against them and the penalties that you impress upon them has grown in their heart more than thinking and worrying that God might tear up the promissory note against them and against every person. They have talked about your abusive acts in their house more than about the great acts of God. They have groaned about you more than they have perceived the great acts of God.

—St. Shenoute the Archimandrite[1]

For this reason I beg you not to accept a corrupt desire from its very beginning. If we do accept it, we must choke its seeds within. But if we are remiss even this far, as the sinful desire goes forth into action we must kill it by confession and tears, by accusing ourselves.

Nothing is so deadly to sin as self-accusation and self-condemnation with repentance and tears. Have you condemned your sin? Put away the burden. Who says this? God Himself who judges us. "Do you first confess your sins, that you may be justified." Why are you ashamed, why do you blush, tell me, to admit your sins? You are not speaking to a human being, are you, who might reproach you? You are not confessing to your fellow servant, are you, who might expose you? No, rather to the Master, who protects and cherishes you, to the physician you are showing your wound. He is not unaware, is He, even if you do not confess, since He understands everything even before it is done? So why do you not confess? The sin does not become more burdensome because of your self-accusation, does it? Rather it becomes easier and lighter. For this reason He wishes you to confess, not in order to punish you, but in order to forgive you: not I order that He may learn your sin (how could that be, since He knows already?), but in order that you may learn how great a debt He forgives you.

—St. John Chrysostom[2]

CHAPTER FIVE

LiteraLly: The Patriarch and the Tanner

We started our Lenten journey together at the foot of a mountain, well before the beginning of Lent. We started, knowing that scaling this mountain would be difficult, but all we needed to do was show up willing to make the climb. So too, the very first Gospel reading in the Coptic Orthodox Lenten lectionary speaks of mountains—but in a different way. The Vespers Gospel reading for the Sunday of Preparation Week is Mark 11:22–26, which speaks not of climbing mountains, but of moving them.

A word of explanation: in the Coptic Orthodox Church, the first week of Lent is called Preparation Week, and fasting begins that Monday, though the Lent lectionary starts Saturday. In the Eastern Orthodox Church, this week is called "Cheesefare Week." Depending on where the dates fall on the different calendars for the Feast of the Resurrection, Catholic and Protestant Ash Wednesday often falls on Wednesday of this week or the following one.

Now, if I ever do need to get on the other side of a mountain, I'd much rather move it than climb it. And as I'm sure the manual for how to climb a mountain tells us all about the tools we need and the attitude we should have to approach the task with, so too with the lectionary for that first week of Lent: it tells us what we need if we want to move a mountain.

> So Jesus answered and said to them, "Have faith in God. For assuredly, I say to you, whoever says to this mountain, 'Be removed and be cast into the sea,' and does not doubt in his heart, but believes that those things he says will be done, he will have whatever he says." (Mark 11:22–23)

Most Biblical commentaries on this verse consider these words about moving mountains figuratively. St. John Cassian focuses on the immovable confidence we should have in prayer: "While we are praying, there should be no hesitation that would intervene or break down the confidence of our petition by any shadow of despair."[1] St. John Chrysostom highlights the power of prayer to do impossible things:

> The power of prayer has subdued the strength of fire, bridled the rage of lions, silenced anarchy, extinguished wars, appeased the elements, expelled demons, burst the chains of death, enlarged the gates of heaven, relieved diseases, averted frauds, rescued cities from destruction, stayed the sun in its course, and arrested the progress of the thunderbolt.[2]

No less miraculous than moving mountains, Chrysostom's examples draw directly from examples in Scripture of what prayer has done.

However, there are two stories in church history in which prayer miraculously moves an actual, physical mountain. The first is the third-century St. Gregory the Wonderworker, who moved a mountain that was standing in the way of building a church.[3] We don't have many more details about this instance of mountain moving, but we do have much more information about the second story: the moving of the mountain of Muqattam in Cairo, Egypt.

The story takes place in tenth-century Egypt, during the early ruling period of the Fatimids, a dynasty of Ismai'li Muslim rulers in North Africa from 969–1171. The first Fatimid ruler, the Caliph al-Mu'izz li-Din Allah, held a particularly pluralistic court, in which Muslim, Jewish, and Christian Egyptians held influential government positions.[4] According to Coptic historian Iris Habib El-Masri, al-Mu'izz also "had a leaning towards mysticism" and enjoyed hosting religious debates as well as readings from various sacred texts, including the Christian New Testament.[5] In addition to many Christian advisors, the Coptic Orthodox Pope Abraham (Abraam, not to be confused with St. Abraam of Fayoum, nor with Abraham of Genesis) had a good relationship with the ruler.

One of the Caliph's advisors, a Jewish convert to Islam, attempts to increase his influence on al-Mu'izz and decrease the influence of the Christians. So he tells the Caliph of the verse about moving mountains by faith (Matthew 17:20 and Mark 11:23) and asks al-Mu'izz to challenge Pope Abraham with it. The idea of having a mountain moved appeals to the Caliph, who sees it as an opportunity to expand his new capital city of Cairo. So he summons the Patriarch and tells him to "prove the soundness" of the biblical saying or expect persecution of the Christians. Pope Abraham asks the Caliph for three days to pray and return to him.

After three days and nights of fervent fasting and prayer, Pope Abraham sees a vision of the Holy Virgin Mary, who instructs him to take the road to the market and search for a one-eyed man carrying a waterpot on his shoulder. "She instructed Abba Abraam to tell him that he was the man designated by God to perform this sign," according to the Coptic Orthodox Synaxarion, which commemorates this miracle twice on the liturgical calendar.

This man, Samaan (Simeon) works as a laborer in a tannery and lives a simple life on the outskirts of the city. He has one eye because he took Matthew 5:29 literally: he once looked at a woman lustfully and took the awl he used to tan hides and poked out his left eye. He bears a waterpot because he takes Matthew 10:42 literally: every day he distributes water to those who cannot fetch it for themselves—the sick and the elderly—and those who cannot pay the "wages of the water-carrier." This is the kind of person who can help the church face this challenge of physically moving a mountain by faith—someone who takes the words of Christ to mean exactly what he said, both in his personal piety and in his interactions with his neighbors. Someone literally righteous.

The story continues thus:

> The father, the Patriarch, took him along with some of the priests, monks and people to see El-Mu'izz, who was out with the government leaders and the nobles of the city nearby the Mukatam Mountain. The father, the Patriarch, stood with those who were with him on one side and El-Mu'izz and his entourage stood on the other side. The father, the Patriarch, and the believers prayed and knelt down three times, and every time they knelt, they said,

"Kirya-layson" Lord have mercy. Whenever the Patriarch and the
congregation lifted up their heads after each bow, the mountain
would lift up and when they bowed down, the mountain was
lowered down to the ground, and whenever they walked, the
mountain moved before them.[6]

Yes, by their faithful prayers of "Lord, have mercy," the mountain
moves, three times, before the eyes of everyone who has gathered
there, including the Caliph al-Mu'izz. Some believe that the
mountain may have been named "Moqattam," which in Arabic itself
means "broken off," because of this occurrence. In recognition of this
great miracle and because he fears God, al-Mu'izz asks the Patriarch
to request anything he wants; the Pope only requests permission
to rebuild the crumbling church and monastery compound of St.
Mercurius, which still stands today in Old Cairo. The request indeed
echoes the reason St. Gregory moved a mountain centuries before:
to build a church. Receiving permission to restore a non-Muslim
house of worship in Egypt under Islamic rule during this period
was as difficult as moving a mountain. Yet the miracle of moving
the mountain makes this miracle of restoring the church possible,
and the Caliph not only agrees, but offers to pay for the restoration,
which the Patriarch refuses. The permission is enough.

The manual for moving a mountain in this story seems to be: 1)
be challenged to do so by a political authority or face persecution;
2) fast and pray fervently for three days; 3) receive an apparition
from the Theotokos instructing you to find a specific person on the
outskirts of the city who takes every word of the Bible literally, even
when it is meant to be figurative; 4) go to the mountain with him
and pray for it to move by asking God's mercy; and 5) watch the
mountain move as Jesus promised.

Considering the general Patristic consensus is that we are not
meant to take Christ's words about moving mountains, plucking out
our eyes, or cutting off our hands literally, Pope Abraham's response
to this challenge teaches us a few things. First, this patriarch did
not try to answer al-Mu'izz or his advisor right away, although he
likely also had faith, being known as a pious and God-fearing man.
He didn't want to put God to the test; rather, he asked for time.

Literally: The Patriarch and the Tanner

In his fervent prayers about the issue, he didn't ask for a miracle, but for discernment. What should he do? He received a divine response, but it wasn't, "Go ahead, show them what you've got," but rather, "Go find a poor, unknown laborer who has more faith than you do, and he will help you." The patriarch showed humility here: rather than protesting, wondering why he, the head of the church, was not enough for this task, he went to the outskirts to find the simple lay person who could help him, and did what he was told. Finally, he obeyed. Praying again, he and St. Samaan moved the mountain. While these days, we are not often challenged by political authorities to prove the veracity of Scripture on pain of persecution, the Muqattam Mountain story assures us that faithful prayers have already indeed moved mountains.[7]

Thus, what we should take literally is the "faith" part of Mark 11. Even if we are not challenged to move Mount Everest, we are called to have the kind of faith that can. To find out how, we need to return to our Lenten mountain-climbing (or mountain-moving) manual, the lectionary. As we face the mountain of Lent, the tools we need to move it are given to us in the readings for the rest of Preparation Week. And if we are not to cut our arms off literally, we are to do one thing very much literally: forgive each other. The very next verse in the mountain moving chapter, Mark 11, Jesus tells us, in verse 25, "and whenever you stand praying, if you have anything against anyone, forgive him, that your Father in heaven may also forgive you your trespasses." Forgiving others is the first step towards faith strong enough to move mountains. If our prayers aren't moving mountains, it's because we haven't overcome the obstacles on the way to the foot of the mountain. The most important obstacle to overcome is forgiving those who have wronged us.

The start of Lent in Eastern traditions is inextricably tied to forgiveness. This contrasts a bit with the start of Lent in the West, with a stronger focus on personal repentance and penance. In the Eastern Orthodox tradition, believers attend a "Forgiveness Vespers" at the end of which every congregation member approaches the priest and asks, "Forgive me, I a sinner," and the priest responds, "God forgives, I forgive."

While we don't have a Forgiveness Vespers in the Coptic Orthodox Church, we do begin Preparation Week with the Sunday Gospel in which Jesus teaches his apostles to pray. In Matthew 6:9–14 Christ says, "In this manner, therefore, pray," and then teaches them the now familiar Lord's Prayer:

Our Father in heaven,
Hallowed be Your name.
Your kingdom come.
Your will be done
On earth as it is in heaven.
Give us this day our daily bread.
And forgive us our debts,
As we forgive our debtors.
And do not lead us into temptation,
But deliver us from the evil one.
For Yours is the kingdom and the power and the glory forever.
Amen.

We have perhaps become so accustomed to these words that sometimes, we fail to take them as seriously and literally as they were meant to be taken. How many of us have prayed these words glibly while still holding a grudge against a brother or sister? In a sermon on this Sunday Gospel, St. Fr. Bishoy Kamel gave an example from the life of St. Abraam of Fayoum to demonstrate the seriousness of these words we pray daily. St. Abraam once tried to mediate between two people who were in conflict. They could not forgive each other, and when the bishop saw that they were getting nowhere, he decided to conclude the meeting and asked the two people to stand up to pray. As they prayed the Lord's Prayer, when they got to "and forgive us our debts," he stopped them. He refused to allow them to continue the prayer and told them they could not pray this part of it. God's forgiveness for us is tied to our forgiveness of others. The people who were in conflict learned the lesson from St. Abraam and forgave each other. They feared for their salvation and acted accordingly.

Although the Coptic Orthodox Church does not have a Forgiveness Vespers ritual, in some villages in Egypt, on this Sunday that begins Preparation Week, each member of the congregation approaches the priest after the liturgy to ask him this question, "Am I worthy to fast?" The priest would usually respond yes. There was only one case in which a priest would tell a villager that they were not worthy to fast—if they were in an argument with someone and had not forgiven them. In those small Egyptian villages where everyone knows everyone, the priest would know about such a dispute. And because no one wanted to be embarrassed in front of everyone on Sunday with the words "No, you are not worthy," they made sure to seek and offer forgiveness before that day.

These villagers understand the climb rightly. They know they are heading towards a great spiritual struggle. Rather than bemoan the difficulties to come, they ask something different—am I worthy to embark on this path to the mountain? Am I worthy to get started on this climb? And the answer to that question is not whether the villagers have prayed all the hours or attended all the church services, but whether the villagers have forgiven anyone who wronged them.

This repeated insistence on forgiveness in Scripture and in Lenten tradition can mean only one thing—it is difficult, as difficult as moving a mountain. Forgiveness might itself be this mountain we need to move by faith. The requirement of forgiveness, when understood in the Middle Eastern context, makes it even more radical. Although rare in the twenty-first century, in some of Egypt's southern villages there persists a terrible extrajudicial tradition called *thar* (pronounced *ttar*). Two clans might have *thar* between them, which means that they have a generational blood "vendetta"—sometimes long after the reason for the original dispute has been forgotten. But if the original dispute resulted in someone's death, then that person's family must protect their honor by killing a male member of the perpetrator's clan. Once this happens, though, the other family becomes honor-bound to seek vengeance for their dead, so the blood feud between the families continues, generation after generation.[8] A decision to forgive rather than to uphold the vendetta means culturally dishonoring the family. Forgiveness in this context can have negative social repercussions. A decision to seek forgiveness can also have negative and even fatal consequences.

A *thar* can end when one side admits to weakness and asks the other side to forgive and end the vendetta. The side that admits to weakness not only faces social dishonor but possible death at the hands of the other side—on their way to seeking forgiveness.

Scripture attests to this kind of clan vengeance culture in the ancient Near East because Mosaic law created prohibitions around it. Numbers 35:19 stipulates that the "avenger of blood" may kill the murderer of someone from his family, but only the murderer and not a substitute kinsman. This indicates that there indeed was a social culture surrounding the Israelites that allowed for (or expected) the death of a substitute in place of the murdered person. Scripture also allows for the perpetrator of manslaughter to escape to a city of refuge, where the blood avenger is not allowed to go to exact vengeance. If that perpetrator leaves the city of refuge earlier than the prescribed time and the blood avenger hears about it, the blood avenger may kill the perpetrator. These laws limited this kind of vengeance while acknowledging the existence of these kinds of clan feuds. They were written in a region at a time when blood feuds like the one I described above were common.[9]

While such notions of cultural honor and vengeance may seem foreign to those of us who do not live in these contexts, it remains that forgiveness can still be difficult for us. And Christ speaking of forgiveness isn't just about forgiveness of grave offenses like murder, but all the kinds of ways we can hurt or injure one another, too. Forgiving those who have wronged us may also have negative social repercussions. We might be seen as weak by offering forgiveness instead of exacting revenge or demanding repayment for wrongs. We might need to swallow our personal pride to offer forgiveness. If we delay forgiveness towards a person or group that has wronged us, our state of unforgiveness might start to meld itself into our personal identities, affect our ongoing relationships, and make it even harder to forgive, because forgiving means changing our identities.

We might know a person who has defined themselves by a grievance, who has lived their life in bitterness, angry at the person (or a group) who wronged them, angry at God or the universe for being wronged. The scary neighbor in the original *Home Alone* movie is an example of this: estranged from his son, he lives as a recluse who rarely speaks to anyone. His entire demeanor changes when—spoiler alert—he finally calls his son and they reconcile. Some define themselves by their anger towards their parents, making life decisions sometimes just to eke out their own personal revenge, even when the parent is deceased. In the first book of a wildly popular regency romance series, the central conflict between the duke and his wife, the viscount's daughter, is that the duke does not want to have children out of revenge on his father, who—spoiler alert—belittled and neglected him because of his stutter so much that the duke wanted his father's title to end in his generation. Although the book doesn't use the word *forgiveness*, the duke's marital relationship with the viscount's daughter is doomed to failure if the duke does not let go of his anger towards his deceased father. His biggest difficulty in letting go is how much that anger integrates itself into his identity and his life narrative. Forgiveness means changing himself.

These pop culture examples are illustrative of many lived realities. While some of us might hold petty grudges we refuse to let go of, others of us have real grievances that run so deep that they may have caused us irreparable harm. The imprint of some life traumas can make forgiveness even more challenging, because the difficult work of forgiveness might mean reliving some of those traumas. In these cases, spiritual and therapeutic guidance is advised.

Forgiveness is made more challenging by some of our misconceptions about it. The most important misconception about forgiveness is that it should come easily and naturally, especially if we are Christians, even for the gravest of crimes against us. We often marvel at stories of inconceivable forgiveness while forgetting the difficult work it takes to get to that point. Author Sophfronia Scott provides an important example. Scott's son Tain survived the Sandy Hook Elementary massacre in 2012 but lost his best friend and godbrother, among the twenty children and seven adults killed that day. Like many parents, Scott spent most of that terrible day waiting to find out if her son would come home from school alive, and then the rest of the night mourning the best friend and classmates he lost. On a podcast interview over a decade later, Scott talked about an essay she wrote about the importance of forgiveness, explaining that "the reason I could write about forgiveness then is because my personal experience goes way back to learning how to forgive my father."[10] In order to have the ability to forgive the perpetrator of the massacre for a crime of such magnitude, Scott had to first learn how to forgive the people in her life who she felt had wronged her in more everyday, yet still painful ways.

Required to write an autobiographical essay for class in college, Scott had to first remember and confront the ways her father had hurt her, like hitting her and her sisters to discipline them, being excessively strict, and demeaning them with his words. Scott's college roommate asked her to consider why her father might have raised her and her sister this way. Scott had not considered the possibility that his behaviors came from a place of love, and when she did take the time to consider it, this changed her life. "This wasn't an easy thing to accept, sure, but when I got to that point something in me shifted. I felt it. I knew this was a seminal moment in my life."[11] Despite leaving her Ohio home for Harvard angry and resolved never to return, Scott confronted her anger with her father and all the ways he had wronged her. She looked at life through his experiences, recognized the real fears that drove him as an African American father to parent his daughters the way he did, and was able to go home for the holidays able to forgive him and to sit with him, knowing that she was loved.

That's how Scott could later forgive Sandy Hook shooter Adam Lanza. Her path to forgiveness demonstrates how forgiveness is less of a feeling and more of a practice, one that must be practiced on smaller things before being tapped into for bigger things. It also demonstrates that forgiveness is not forgetting. Forgiveness actually begins with remembering and confronting the wrongs done to us. Forgiveness may not necessarily lead to us forgetting those wrongs, but it will lead us to us removing them from actively playing a role in our thoughts, emotions, and behaviors.

In fact, the popular phrase "forgive and forget," which gets repeated often in Christian circles, never actually appears in Scripture. Although it is perhaps an interpretation of Micah

Literally: The Patriarch and the Tanner

7:19, "You will cast all our sins into the depths of the sea," or Psalm 103:12, "As far as the east is from the west, So far has He removed our transgressions from us," in both cases, it is only God who forgives in this way. Asking someone who has been through war, persecution, abuse, or other forms of trauma to "forgive and forget" is like asking them to remove brain cells. When Christ asks us to forgive in the Lord's Prayer, he isn't asking us to forget. He's asking us to remember that we, too, have been forgiven, and to act accordingly.

The second common misconception about forgiveness is that forgiveness means reconciliation and restoration of relationships. These are three different things, and although forgiveness is the prerequisite to reconciliation and restoration, reconciliation and restoration are not required for forgiveness, nor are they necessarily recommended in many situations. We are called to forgive those who have wronged us in all situations, but reconciliation and restoration only have a place in certain relationships. For example, it's important for me to forgive my children (and ask their forgiveness), reconcile with them, and restore our loving relationship with each other as a family. It is not so necessary with a colleague at work or a classmate at school or even a fellow parishioner at church. And even in some cases within families where physical, verbal, and psychological abuse have occurred, reconciliation and restoration might not be healthy or safe.

In *From Red Earth: A Rwandan Story of Healing and Forgiveness*, Denise Uwimana chronicles the healing work she did with the surviving women in the wake of the Rwandan Genocide. Over 100 days in 1994, neighbor turned against neighbor in a horrific conflict during which the Hutu Rwandans killed one million Tutsi Rwandans. The work Uwimana did with the Tutsi "genocide widows"—women who had lost their families during the war—spanned over 25 years. As they struggled to heal from the devastating trauma and rebuild their lives, they also had to decide what to do about their anger towards the people responsible for murdering their families. Six years after the genocide, Uwimana's friend Beata Mukarubuga received a letter from prison. In the letter, her former neighbor Manasseh Nshimyerugira confessed to killing five of her children and to having nightmares about what he did every night for all those years. He pleaded for her forgiveness, but Mukarubuga could not offer it, not for someone who had killed her children in cold blood. However, she also began having nightmares. "Beata's heart," Uwimana writes, "became a war zone, justice fighting mercy."

The internal war escalated when Nshimyerugira sent her another letter with information about the location of her children's bodies. This letter triggered Mukarubuga's traumatic memories of those days, yet it also helped her have closure when she searched for the mass grave, found her children's remains, and gave them a proper burial. Two years later, Mukarubuga decided to visit Nshimyerugira in prison. There, allowing Christ to win the war in her heart, she decided to forgive him. Forgiving him for her did not mean she could ever forget what happened to her family. In her words, "Forgiveness is a choice, an attitude to life. It's a decision I have to affirm every day, with God's help. Because when I wake up each morning, my husband and children are still dead."[12]

Although Mukarubuga greets Nshimyerugira whenever she sees him now, forgiving him does not mean they became best friends. There are other stories in Uwimana's book where profound reconciliation does happen between the perpetrators of the genocide and the survivors, but these are exceptions, not rules. In 2017, the wife of Naseem Faheem astounded all the Egyptians watching on national television when she announced that she forgave the suicide bomber who killed her husband as he redirected the bomber through the metal detector at St. Mark's Cathedral in Alexandria. The so-called Islamic State of Iraq and Syria (ISIS) claimed responsibility for this and another Palm Sunday bombing, and while Faheem's widow said, "I'm not angry at the one who did this. I'm telling him, 'May God forgive you, and we also forgive you. Believe me, we forgive you,'" she was not inviting the terrorists back to Alexandria for tea.[13] She was inviting them to repent and receive God's forgiveness.

Similarly, after Dylan Roof entered Emanuel AME Church in Charleston, South Carolina, and killed nine people during Bible study, several family members of the victims announced their

Literally: The Patriarch and the Tanner

forgiveness of Roof, a self-proclaimed white supremacist—including the pastor of the church, whose wife was among the nine killed. For these families, forgiveness does not necessarily mean that Roof will be invited to supper in their homes or babysit their grandchildren. It means, to again quote Sophfronia Scott,

> We need to forgive so we can still have a vision of a better world. The shootings in Sandy Hook and now Charleston are grim reminders that we are far from it, but not forgiving will take us even further away. We would remain stuck. We would remain traumatized, whether we realize it or not. Unless we choose to be the light in the world, as Ms. Collier and others like her have done, we succumb to the darkness. When we don't forgive, the victim count grows, and can grow exponentially. Adam Lanza took twenty-seven. Dylann Roof took nine. They don't get to take any more. That's why forgiveness matters.[14]

Forgiveness provides peace and a more abundant life to the forgiver, regardless of the contrition of the wrongdoer. Forgiveness allows Christians to continue to shine light to the world, to show that such a light is possible even in the midst of the darkest suffering. Forgiveness can even undo the evil that was attempted by the perpetrator in the first place. Charles Singleton, whose mother died in the Charleston shooting, believes that forgiving Roof meant doing the opposite of what Roof wanted to do with the shooting—start a race war. By forgiving him, their community did not allow him to succeed.[15]

The various translations of the Lord's Prayer become instructive here. In the NKJV translation, Christ says "forgive us our debts, as we have forgiven our debtors." The Book of Common Prayer uses the word "trespasses" rather than debts. The word "debts," which is closest to the Greek word used in the New Testament, recalls the parable of the debtors in Luke 7:41–43 (NASB):

> "A moneylender had two debtors: the one owed five hundred denarii, and the other, fifty. When they were unable to repay, he canceled the debts of both. So which of them will love him more?" Simon answered and said, "I assume the one for whom he canceled the greater debt." And He said to him, "You have judged correctly."

The context of this parable makes it clear that God is the "moneylender," and the two debtors represent two different categories of sinners: the ones whose sins are great, and the ones whose sins are few. In both cases, neither debtor was able to repay, yet both were forgiven. This is the same for us—whether our sins are great in number or whether they are few, we cannot undo those sins. We need forgiveness. And because we have received such limitless forgiveness, we must also forgive one another "seventy times seven." The survivors of the Sandy Hook massacre, the Emanuel Church shooting, and the Coptic Orthodox church bombings who forgave recognized that the forgiveness they have already received from God is greater than the forgiveness they could offer to the perpetrators of those awful crimes committed against them.

The Greek language has a word for sin (a word whose literal meaning is "missing the mark"), but our Lord Jesus does not use this word in the Lord's Prayer. He uses "debt" and "debtor" instead. According to Orthodox Biblical scholar Dr. Jeannie Constantinou, this is because the words "debt" and "debtor" are *relational*. "If you owe a debt it's because you have some kind of relationship with the other person," she says.[16] And in the Lord's Prayer, forgiveness is not just something between an individual and God, but between an individual, God, and others.

The words "debt" and "debtor" also recall a concept we discussed in an earlier chapter—Jubilee. During the year of Jubilee, all debts were forgiven, and the ancient Israelites returned to their original inheritance—an inheritance won for them by God's promise, not by their own might or even their own righteousness. They had, as a people, demonstrated faithlessness and idolatry during their forty-year wandering in the desert on their way to the Promised Land. If they lent money, they had to forgive those debts during the year of Jubilee, for they also were indebted to God's favor to them.

The Book of Common Prayer translates "forgive us our debts" as "forgive us our trespasses," and the use of this translation remains common in churches today. Although the word "trespass" does not mean debt, it is a similarly relational word. The definition of trespassing at the time of the Book of Common Prayer's publication in the sixteenth century includes "transgression," but its definition also includes land and property. A "trespasser" can be someone who enters another person's private property without permission. Trespassing involves others. In the year of Jubilee, an Israelite who bought another Israelite's property had to return that property to them according to the original tribal inheritance. The trespasser on that property today might be the owner of that property tomorrow. And the owner received that property not by purchasing it, but by being granted an inheritance. We too, as Christians, have been granted an eternal inheritance we did not purchase or deserve. So we, too, should forgive those who have "trespassed against us," since what we have was granted to us by God in the first place.

Christ calls us to forgive as we have been forgiven, not only because of God's infinite forgiveness, but also because through his coming he has done more than forgive us. We are called to forgive, but he came to forgive us of our sins, to reconcile us with God, and to restore us to our original image. Forgiveness is difficult, yes, but Christ only asks us to forgive, while he does the rest through his incarnation, his cross, and his resurrection. So we begin Lent with forgiveness, and we travel through Lent and Holy Week to the cross and the Resurrection to commemorate the reconciliation and restoration Christ has accomplished for us.

That Sunday before Lent, when we are supposed to finally remove from our homes all the food we aren't supposed to eat during Lent, we are also called to rid ourselves of the anger and bitterness that keep us from loving our neighbor by lifting that unforgiveness up to God. Then, the door opens to reconciliation and restoration. Then, we get a little bit closer to the kind of faith that moves mountains.

1. Who are the people in our lives we need to forgive? What work do we need to do to genuinely offer that forgiveness?

2. How does our understanding of forgiveness change when we separate it from reconciliation and restoration?

3. How does forgiveness relate to our hunger and thirst for righteousness?

CHAPTER SIX

TAKE AND READ: ABBA SERAPION

There's another side to the forgiveness equation, of course. That is the side of asking for forgiveness. And if forgiving someone who has wronged you is difficult, asking forgiveness is even more difficult. Asking forgiveness is acknowledging you did something wrong *in the first place*. This isn't comfortable, and most of us do all that we can to avoid it. Our knee-jerk reaction to any accusation of wrongdoing is often denial (hence the phrase "denial isn't just a river in Egypt"). Recognizing our wrongdoing requires reflection, self-evaluation, and humility. Hence, the season of Lent is also the season of repentance—repentance, however, not just between each individual one of us and God, but between us as a community and God, and between us and the others we have wronged.

We often think of repentance and confession as individual endeavors, but Lent reminds us that repentance cannot be a solitary act. The church calls all of us to turn to God and away from sin during this season of repentance. It calls us to do so collectively, the way Nineveh repented—with fasting and prayer at the same time, together. And while confession might happen individually, the church encourages everyone to use this season of collective repentance as an opportunity to confess our sins and receive forgiveness.

It's easy to overlook that the calls to repentance in the Old Testament were God's calls to a people, a whole community, who had abandoned him. For the Israelites to turn to God and avoid his wrath, they had to do so as a nation, not as separate, individual people. God was willing to save Sodom and Gomorrah if there were ten righteous men—in other words, if there were a community, an assembly of people living righteously in the midst of an evil city. God would save Lot and his family from the destruction of Sodom, but in order to save Sodom as a whole, there needed to be a community of righteous people, not just one or two.

Our hyper-individualized Western mindset might find this strange, but what is actually strange is our hyper-individualized mentality as Christians. We are indeed each children of God, created in the image of God, each individually and personally loved by God, but we are also created for community and relationship. God is in himself relationship as Father, Son, and Holy Spirit. As persons made in the image of God, we can and should worship God individually, but our most important act of worship is as a community in the Eucharist. We should repent individually throughout the year, but during the season of Lent we repent together. Hence, the hymn we sing in the Coptic Orthodox Church during Lent, "*We* too should fast: in purity and righteousness: and pray: crying and saying: I have sinned, I have sinned: O my Lord Jesus forgive me," is sung on Sundays, when we are worshiping together. If we seek righteousness individually we might save ourselves; if we seek righteousness as a community we might save the whole city.

Sin is in fact, separation—it is the anti-community. In his book *Return to Me,* His Holiness Pope Shenouda outlines the multiple ways sin is separation: from God, from the community of Saints, from the church. "Return, then, to God," he says, "not for your sake only, but for the sake also of those around you."[1] When we return to God we bring joy to the saints and encouragement to the believers. We complete the community which has felt our loss with the pain a family feels when mourning the emptiness of an estranged child's seat at the table.

Fr. Alexander Schmemann writes in *Great Lent: A School of Repentance*, that during Lent "Not only individuals but the whole Church acquires a penitential spirit."[2] In the Gospel of Luke, the parable of the lost sheep is not just about that one sheep, but about returning that one sheep to the ninety-nine sheep in the fold. Similarly, the parable of the lost coin is not just about the one lost coin, but about returning that one coin so the woman has ten again.

The Fathers point out the significance of the numbers ten and one hundred in the Bible. St. Cyril of Alexandria says of the lost coin, "It is as one out of ten, a perfect number and of a sum complete in the accounting. The number ten is also perfect, being the close of a series from the unit upwards."[3] Similarly, to understand the significance of one hundred in the parable of the lost sheep, we must know something about ancient accounting. In accounting during antiquity, double digit numbers were counted on the left hand, and triple digit numbers on the right hand. Restoring the one to the ninety-nine completes the hundred, and brings the accounting over from the left hand to the right hand:

> Both the Gospel of Truth (explicitly) and Augustine (implicitly) suggest that the return of the lost sheep had efficacious effects for the ninety-nine to whom it was returned. The original number of "one hundred" is now restored, and the community, whose destiny was inextricably tied to the return of the one, can continue to enjoy the benefits of being on the "right side."[4]

Understanding, therefore, that the numbers ten and one hundred in the Bible are symbols of perfection, completion, and wholeness, we can understand that with repentance, the heavens rejoice over the one not just for the sake of the one, but also because the one makes the rest perfect and whole again.

In *Putting Joy into Practice*, I referenced the "rejoicing" in these parables to demonstrate how repentance is a practice that orients us to receiving joy from God because it orients us to God's direction and away our own sins. When we repent together as a faithful community, we don't just experience joy, but we also experience power. In *Taught by God: Making Sense of the Difficult Sayings of Jesus*, Fr. Daniel Fanous draws a connection between repentance and violent power.[5] The unanimous Patristic interpretation of the difficult verse "the kingdom of heaven suffers violence, and the violent take it by force" (Matthew 11:12) comes from their understanding of the Greek word for "suffers violence" as "the one who breaks open." Linking this verse to the prophecy in Micah 2:13 about the restoration of Israel, Fanous explains it through the imagery of sheep penned in at night, getting agitated when they wake up, and pounding against the stones penning them in until one of the sheep "breaks open," and the rest of the sheep "break out" with it. The prophecy reads,

> The one who breaks open will come up before them;
> They will break out,

Pass through the gate,
And go out by it;
Their king will pass before them,
With the Lord at their head.

Jewish biblical commentary identifies "the one who breaks open" as Elijah, the Messiah as king, and the Lord as God. Thus, considering St. John the Baptist came with the spirit of Elijah, it is he who "breaks open" the Kingdom with his message of repentance, and those who heed the call to repentance also "break out" and "pass through the gate" to take the Kingdom of Heaven with violent force. "Indeed the key to the kingdom is repentance so violent," Fanous writes, "that the gates of heaven cannot withstand its force."

The call to repentance here is clearly not just about one person repenting individually, but an entire community—an entire people—rushing forward to take the Kingdom with violent power. "It is only in this violent desire for the kingdom, and thus for God, that man may reach the kingdom," Fanous continues. This violent desire is akin to the kind of hunger and thirst we must have for righteousness—a desire so powerful that, combined with the repentance of those around us, it is like a violent takeover.

If an individual's repentance is like a prison escape, a community's repentance is like a prison break. We are the prisoners, imprisoned by sin, and the church, like St. John the Baptist, "breaks open" the prison doors for us through the Lenten call to repentance. Our powerful tide of repentance does not just help us break out of prison, but, with Christ among us, who is both "Messiah" and "Lord," we get to take over the Kingdom of Heaven. The powerful tide overthrows the tyrannical rule of sin over us, not only freeing us from prison but also giving us the power to take over the entire Kingdom. We can imagine, then, that the heavenly jubilation at our repentance as a community sounds not like a house party, but like the deafening stadium roar at the scoring of a goal by the home team in a final championship game. Powerful.

Thus, Lent serves as the perfect time for non-Christians to prepare for baptism. Although Lent as a fast is largely practiced by people who are already Christian, catechumens—those who are learning about Christianity so that they can be baptized and join the body of believers—also spend the period of Lent repenting of their past sins, turning away from their previous lives, and looking forward to a life in Christ. The season of Lent thus adds more power to the community of believers. More of us repenting means more of us get to take over the Kingdom—and succeed.

Catechumens spend the time of Lent not only repenting but also fasting and reading Scripture. Lots and lots of Scripture. Much of that Scripture can be found in the Lenten daily lectionary. I've mentioned the Lenten lectionary as a "guidebook" for climbing the mountain of Lent, giving us the tools that we need for an acceptable fast. If we consider that it was also the "textbook" for those preparing to be baptized before Easter, then what happens to us during Lent when we read those same Scriptures with open hearts like catechumens is a renewal of our own baptism, our first repentance.

Rereading the same Lenten lectionary every year is not a review for us but a reset—much like the year of Jubilee. As Fr. Alexander Schmemann writes in *Great Lent: Journey to Pascha*,

> For even though we are baptized, what we constantly lose and
> betray is precisely that which we received at Baptism. Therefore
> Easter is our return every year to our own Baptism, whereas Lent
> is our preparation for that return—the slow and sustained effort to
> perform, at the end, our own "passage" or "pascha" into the new life
> in Christ.[6]

Just as many Israelites may have lost parts of their original inheritance during the years between the years of Jubilee, so we too may lose over time parts of the inheritance we received at our Baptism. Rather than waiting an entire generation, however, to regain the inheritance, we need only wait until the next Lent to prepare for the Jubilee and regain the new life in Christ he gave us in our baptism through his resurrection.

At a recent exhibition at the Metropolitan Museum of Art, I beheld a priceless twelfth-century manuscript, the "Pentaglot Psalter." The psalms in this Psalter are inscribed by hand in five different languages: Coptic, Arabic, Syriac, Ethiopic, and Armenian. The ink is clearly of high quality, using a red color very expensive to obtain at that time, and written on parchment, a type of paper made of animal hide. Despite its high monetary value, the smudges on the ink and the frayed edges indicate its regular use. It could have been used in prayer at a monastery that might have had monks speaking several different languages praying together. It could have been made available to accommodate visitors from within and outside of Egypt looking to study. It could have been made available to pilgrims traveling through Wadi el-Natrun, Egypt, and using it for prayer. Bound at the Monastery of the three Macarii (Deir Abu-Makar), it was likely used at St. Mary's Monastery of the Syrians (Deir el-Suryan). The Met had the manuscript on loan from the Vatican.

How would this valuable Egyptian multilingual manuscript end up at the Vatican? Well, in the seventeenth century, a Catholic priest in Egypt saw it and recognized its value, only to discover he couldn't buy it for the French art collector he had in mind. For the monastery, this manuscript belonged to its endowment and could not be sold for money. It could only be traded for another sacred object. The manuscript's worth did not just lie in its high monetary value, but in its use for prayer and study of Scripture. So Anba Yunus, the metropolitan of the Monastery of St. Macarius, traded the manuscript for a silver paten and chalice—for altar vessels to be used during the Divine Liturgy. The manuscript was shipped to France, but on its way it was "rerouted through unknown hands and unknown means."[7] Legend has it that pirates attacked the ship in the Mediterranean sea and stole everything on it. Somehow, the Psalter found its way to an art collector in Tripoli before it was purchased by the Grand Master of the Knights of Malta. He gave it as a gift to Cardinal Barberini's library, and then from there it eventually moved to the Vatican Library.[8]

Now that we can read Scripture in almost any medium and access it almost anywhere, that all seems to be a lot of effort for a book of psalms. It helps to remember that in the twelfth century, only the wealthy could afford to own a copy of the Bible in their homes. Bishops, monks, and other clergy had access only if a literate monk could hand-copy it, or if a wealthy person commissioned a copy for them. In the twelfth century, the books of Scripture were considered as important and as holy as the vessels on the altar that held the body and blood of Jesus Christ for communion. Yet what made them holy and important then are what make them holy and important now: the words of the Scripture itself.

Perhaps, then, we should regard the multiple printed copies of Scripture we may keep at home in addition to the ebook and Bible apps we have in our pockets as a sign of great wealth. For the only way the common people had access to those Scriptures in the twelfth century was to go to church and hear them being read.

Fortunately for them and for us, the church has always been generous with its reading of Scripture, especially during Lent. During most services in the Orthodox church, we read five biblical passages: a selection from the epistle of St. Paul (the Pauline epistles), a selection from the epistles of Peter, James, John, or Jude (the Catholic epistles), a selection from the Acts of the Apostles, a few verses from the Psalms, and a Gospel reading. During Lent, the Coptic Orthodox Church's Lenten lectionary is particularly extensive, adding to these several long selections from the Old Testament. The Holy Week lectionary is so exhaustive it takes at least three hours in the morning and three hours in the evening to read.

These extensive readings served two important purposes. First, they served as a kind of Christianity 101 for the catechumens— individuals who were preparing themselves for baptism. Lent served, and continues to serve, as a preparation period for baptism in many church traditions. The Catholic Church, for example, has three Sundays during Lent called "Scrutinies," with special readings for those adults preparing for baptism. In the Eastern Orthodox Church, catechumens were often baptized on Bright Saturday. In the Coptic Orthodox Church, baptisms were (and still are) done on the weekend of "hadd el nassarra"—the Sunday of Becoming Christian—which is also the last Sunday of Lent, before Palm

Sunday. In all cases, this allowed the newly baptized to participate in Holy Communion in time for the Feast of the Resurrection. Second, the readings provided spiritual food for believers during a time of abstinence from physical food.

The church during Lent thus encourages us to return to the regular reading of Scripture during this season. And as we have been given the gift of greater access to Scripture than the early Christians did, so our responsibility increases. Scripture serves as our main spiritual food during Lent, and Lent serves as our opportunity to build an ongoing daily spiritual practice of reading Scripture that lasts even after the fasting period ends.

For Christians in America, if we are not regularly reading the Bible, we sadly belong to the majority. According to the Pew Research Center's 2014 Religious Landscape Study, only thirty-five percent of American adults read Scripture more than once a week. Eighteen percent read it once a month or once a year, and forty-five percent read it seldom or never.[9] I will be the first to confess that I often fall off my daily Bible reading habit. My temptation is an attraction to new books over Scripture I've already read. Even if those books are religious in nature, they are still distractions preventing me from reading the word of Life itself.

Reading the Bible can seem like an overwhelming endeavor, especially if we have attempted to read it from cover to cover and then summarily abandoned the task, usually at the book of Leviticus. We often get discouraged by this kind of reading because we don't understand what we read, are troubled by what we read because we have no context for it, or find detailed genealogies and tabernacle building instructions tedious and uninspiring.

So, some of us read selections from the Bible in a shallow way, using the popular "quiet time" method, reading popular short passages and looking for God's personal message to us specifically relevant to our daily lives, even if those passages are chosen at random. However, "the way daily quiet time is typically practiced today," according to Bible scholars Durgin and Johnson, "is unlikely to yield the fluency required to understand and apply biblical teaching."[10] Because these random passages are read out of context (or are chosen within devotionals based on themes like God's promises for our lives), Durgin and Johnson suggest Christians look to the longer-standing Catholic contemplative practice of *lectio divina*, which has some of its origins in the contemplative Scripture reading practices of the early Desert Fathers.

Lectio divina, Latin for "divine reading," follows a sequence of meditative practices for reading a biblical passage: *lectio* (reading), *meditatio* (meditation), *oratio* (prayer), and *contemplatio* (contemplation). Many books and resources exist for learning more about this practice, covering those four aspects of it. However, a less practiced but essential fifth aspect of *lectio divina* is *operatio*—the performance of good works. Orthodox biblical scholar Fr. John Breck points out this addition by Hugues San-Victor, noting, "For *lectio* to issue in *contemplatio*, the inner struggle of the reader needs to be coupled with humble service, a genuine *operatio* or *diakonia*, that represents a living participation in Christ's redemptive work for the world's salvation."[11] Most literature explaining the idea of "quiet time" or the process of *lectio divina* rarely incorporates this important aspect of reading Scripture—*diakonia*. Not only is God's Word meant to apply to us and inspire us to contemplation and prayer, but also it is meant for us to act upon it in the service of others.

Still, even this addition of *operatio* to the process of *lectio divina* doesn't address its core challenge for many believers—its very systemized process of steps that, for the uninitiated, can also seem overwhelming. For even though *lectio divina* may have had its roots in the Desert Fathers (as well as some Patristic Fathers), none of the Fathers prescribed something so methodical. The Fathers urged frequent reading of Scripture, memorizing it, studying it, analyzing it, praying with it, applying it, and acting upon it, but not necessarily in any specific order in any one given time.

For the Desert Fathers, according to Dom Armand Veilleux, who translated the great Egyptian Desert Fathers' work the *Pachomian Koinonia*, the idea of *lectio divina* was not a process at all. "The first monks had no method. They had an attitude of reading," he says.[12] Every kind of reading Scripture, whether it is study or contemplative, needed to be approached by the attitude of readiness to be changed by it. Reducing our reading of Scripture to an exercise or ritual during a certain time of day without allowing that reading to transform our actual way of living or being, according to Veilleux, misses the point of reading Scripture altogether.

Lent gives us the opportunity to approach Scripture with a readiness to be changed by it. We are, after all, participating in a season with the desire to be changed, the desire for greater intimacy with God, the desire to love our neighbor as ourselves through good works. And the Church also helps us overcome the challenge of approaching Scripture by giving us a special lectionary during the Lenten season. We can read the daily Lenten lectionary from our respective communions in whole or in part during the season, knowing that we are reading passages set for us not randomly, not by one individual, but by collective ancient church tradition, meant to teach catechumen and baptized believer alike.

The Litany of the Gospel in St. Basil's Liturgy in the Coptic Orthodox Church, prayed by the priest before the reading of the Gospel, offers us a much simpler *lectio divina* to follow during Lent and afterward. A prayer offered in front of the altar while the priest raises incense, it asks God to "make us worthy to hear and act according to the Holy Gospel, through the prayers of the saints." This prayer can help us in our daily personal reading of Scripture, too, because it makes three important requests from God: to make us worthy, to help us hear, and to help us act. The prayer also illuminates the context in which we ought to be reading Scripture, whether it is alone in our rooms or listening audibly during liturgy: the context of the Church.

In this prayer, we ask God first to "make us worthy." Worthiness, of course, is a tricky word here. What makes us worthy? The words preceding "make us worthy" provide us the answer:

> Master, Lord Jesus Christ our God, Who said to His saintly, honored disciples and pure apostles: "Many prophets and righteous men have desired to see the things which you see, and have not seen them, and to hear the things which you hear, and have not heard them. But blessed are your eyes for they see and your ears for they hear."

This verse, from Matthew 13, references a prophecy in Isaiah 6:9–10. God calls Isaiah in this chapter to go and tell the people:

'Keep on hearing, but do not understand;
Keep on seeing, but do not perceive.'
"Make the heart of this people dull,
And their ears heavy,
And shut their eyes;
Lest they see with their eyes,
And hear with their ears,
And understand with their heart,
And return and be healed."

Matthew paraphrases these verses in chapter 13. Isaiah then asks, "Lord, how long?" And the Lord responds, "Until the cities are laid waste and without inhabitant, The houses are without a man, The land is utterly desolate" (6:11). So the people do not hear or understand the message that might cause them to return and be healed until they are laid desolate. Yet we read later in Isaiah 53:8, in his prophecy about the Messiah, that it is the Messiah who will bear these punishments:

He was taken from prison and from judgment,
And who will declare His generation?
For He was cut off from the land of the living;
For the transgressions of My people He was stricken.

We are made worthy to hear and to act according to the Holy Gospel because Christ's coming and taking upon Himself the desolation promised to Israel has allowed us to see and hear. Thus, the first posture of our Scripture reading should be that of those who were made worthy by grace. We are able to see and hear because of Christ's life-giving death for us on the cross.

The Litany goes on, praying for us to be worthy to "hear and act." Let us first focus on the word *hear*. Throughout Scripture, hearing is not just about hearing auditory sound. In the words of Catholic theologian George Leo Haydock, "hear" in Scripture means to listen and "be ready to comply with whatever may be required."[13] Thus when Samuel says to God, "Speak, Lord, for Your servant hears" (1 Samuel 3:10), he is not just saying that he can hear the sound of

God's voice, but that he is ready to comply with whatever he hears God say. When the words "Hear O Israel" are called throughout Scripture, they are not being called so that listeners will stop talking and listen to what is being said. Silence being what is expected, they are called to obey what they hear. And so when the Gospel Litany says, "may we be worthy to hear," we are asking God to help us hear the word in this sense—to help us listen and obey. The English phrase "hear, hear," used when a listener wants to show strong support and agreement with what is being said, comes very close to this meaning of "hear" in the Bible.

The Litany prayer does not just stop at "hear," but asks that we be made worthy "to hear and to act." If we have already established that "hear" means to obey what is heard, then "act" goes beyond simple obedience. "Act" here is the *operatio,* the *diakonia.* In Coptic, the word for "act" here is *eiri,* a word that means to do, to act, and to bear fruit. This is action. Our hearing of Scripture should ultimately lead us to action that bears fruit in the service of our neighbors.

Abba Serapion gives us a colorful example of this hearing and acting in the stories of the Desert Fathers. During cold weather, Abba Serapion meets a poor man with no clothes, and so he gives the naked man his own clothes, saying to himself, "This is Christ." Abba Serapion continues walking, with his small copy of the Gospels his only remaining possession. Recalling the cost of biblical manuscripts during this period, likely the fifth century, what happens next is both astounding and yet consistent with our Orthodox *lectio divina:*

A passer-by, who knows him, asks him: "Abba Serapion, who has taken away your clothes?" And Serapion, showing his Gospel, replies: "This is the one who has taken away my clothes." Serapion then goes to another place and there sees someone who is being taken to prison, because he is unable to pay a debt. Serapion, seized with pity, gives him his Gospel, so that he can sell it and so pay his debt. When Serapion returns to his cell, no doubt shivering, his disciple asks him where his tunic is, and Serapion replies that he has sent it where it is more needed than on his body. To his disciple's second question "And where is your Gospel?" Serapion replies: "I have sold the one who continually told me: 'Sell your goods, and give to the poor' (Lk. 12,33)."[14]

Take and Read: Abba Serapion

Abba Serapion heard the word of Scripture and acted accordingly, giving the Word of God to God Himself, who said, "Assuredly, I say to you, inasmuch as you did it to one of the least of these My brethren, you did it to Me" (Matthew 25:40). He sold his Gospel to fulfill the words of the Gospel.

Finally, this prayer is asked "through the prayers of the saints." This situates us within the church in our reading. For even if we are reading alone in our bedrooms, we are still reading with the church. The Orthodox way of reading Scripture is not only to read it in the church, but also to read it with the church, and with the mind of the church. To quote again Fr. John Breck, "Any 'personal' reading of Scripture, then, takes place within the Church, as a function of the life of the Church. Like prayer, it draws us into a living communion with the universal Body of Christian believers."[15] Thus, when we ask to read Scripture "through the prayers of the saints," we are asking the saints to pray for us to obey what we are reading (which can be difficult sometimes) and to act on what we read (which requires God's grace). The saints' prayers help us read with the mind of the church so that we understand what we read through the Orthodox faith.

I suggest, then, that when we sit to read any portion of Scripture, for any reason, whether it is to memorize a favorite verse or psalm, to study for understanding or for sermon preparation, or for personal contemplation, we precede our reading with the sign of the Cross and this prayer, "may we be made worthy to hear and act according to the Holy Gospel, through the prayers of all the Saints." In this way, we can approach Scripture with a readiness to be transformed by it.

In the Appendix of this book I share the various Scripture references for the Coptic Orthodox daily Lenten lectionary. I urge readers from all communions to find out what their church's Lenten lectionary looks like. While I suggest using the Lenten lectionary to start a daily Scripture reading practice or to change up an already existing Scripture reading practice, this is still a start. After Lent, after the Resurrection, our daily reading should continue. It may return to a plan of reading the Bible from cover to cover, or it may be following a daily reading plan to finish the Bible in one year. And as with any new spiritual habit, whatever path we take should be taken with the guidance of our spiritual fathers.

"Make the reading of the Bible an opportunity for repentance," His Holiness Pope Shenouda writes in his book *The Spiritual Means*.[16] Indeed, repentance is transformation, and if we approach our reading of Scripture with the readiness to be transformed by it, then surely repentance is one of those outcomes. Repentance is powerful, all the more powerful when we do it together in community during Lent. So what is it, then, that we must repent of as a community? We can look to the lectionary to find out.

The Coptic lectionary for the first week of Lent tells us that we must repent of injustice, of not defending the fatherless or the cause of the widow (Isaiah 1:21–23, Tuesday of the first week), that we repent of prejudice against those different from us (Wednesday of the first week, Acts 10), that we repent of pride and idolatry (Thursday of the first week, Isaiah 2:11), that we repent of stealing from the poor (Friday of the first week, Isaiah 3:14). We have amassed excessive wealth, joining "house to house and add field to field" (Tuesday of the second week, Isaiah 5:8). We have exploited laborers and turned away the refugee (Wednesday of the second week, Malachi 3:5). We have been proud, idolizing riches, fame, and influence, and considering ourselves superior to others. We have forgotten the plight of the most marginalized among us—the fatherless and the widow—and we have even, in our greed, stolen from the poor for our own comfort and excess. We have closed our doors to the alien, the refugee, even though we, too, are sojourners on this earth.

Each one of us must consider these calls to repentance from Scripture. Each one of us must ask ourselves: When have we been proud, looking down on groups that do not look like us or behave like us? When have we made comments or jokes about other groups, cultures, or even families that we do not belong to? What have we made our idols that we need to destroy so that we might return to God? Have we placed monetary wealth, physical beauty or strength, entertainment, or political or social influence ahead of our obedience and humility towards God? Have we "plundered the poor," in the words of Isaiah, through our excessive use of fast fashion that thrives on the exploitation of low-paid workers or through our investments in financial institutions that collect interest from those who can't afford it? Have we amassed wealth rather than using our gifts to give to others? Have we closed our homes and communities to those who seek refuge with us and consolation from us?

These are the kinds of questions we must ask ourselves individually before we can look to those around us. We must, however, not stop at repenting of these sins on an individual basis, but discover how we might, as a church, return to God by finding ways to defend the most marginalized in our communities, filling our conversations with love rather than judgment, channeling our resources towards the poor, the refugee, and the alien, and away from activities that serve only to enrich ourselves.

The Coptic Orthodox lectionary is only one of many Lenten lectionaries. Read the one from your own tradition every day this season and examine it for the ways it calls us as a community to repent, to return to God, to transform ourselves. Do not be discouraged by the wrongs we have done but be encouraged by the joy we will receive and the power we will have when we repent of those wrongs.

QUESTIONS FOR REFLECTION AND ACTION:
1. Who are the people from whom we should ask forgiveness this Lent? How do we plan on asking forgiveness in a way that doesn't reopen old wounds and cause further drama?
2. How can we characterize our habit of reading Scripture?
3. After Lent is over, how do we plan on continuing our reading of Scripture on a daily basis?

CHAPTER SEVEN

PAYING DEBTS: ST. PAËSIA AND ST. JOHN THE LITTLE

The scene opens with Simon in a bloody fist fight. He and his brother Andrew are in desperate straits, with taxes in arrears and debts to pay. Fishing isn't bringing in enough income, so Simon descends into greater and greater desperation, betting on fights, gambling at bars, fishing on the Sabbath, and even spying for the Romans against his own fellow fishermen. If they cannot pay their debts, under Roman Palestine's harsh laws, Simon and his family can lose their fishing boat, perhaps even their homes, and live as beggars. Worse, if their properties don't cover their debts, they can be sold into slavery, tortured in debtor's prison, or killed.[1] So begins the first episode of the historical fiction television series *The Chosen*, about Christ's disciples. While *The Chosen* has taken plenty of creative liberties with history, the portrayal of the level of desperation into which a Jew in first-century Roman Palestine would fall to pay debt is spot on.

The weight of debt and its consequences on the Roman Empire's lower classes was so great that one historian wrote that "it was safer for a plebeian to face the enemy in war than his own countrymen in time of peace."[2] Some of Rome's earlier laws even allowed creditors to cut off portions of debtor's bodies if they did not pay their debts within a prescribed timeframe.[3] In other words, for the Romans, "debt" and "death" were often synonymous. Hence, when Christ taught the disciples the Lord's Prayer, the verse "forgive us our debts" carried a meaning more powerful than we can imagine. Under the Roman Empire, debt forgiveness wasn't just a financial transaction. Debt forgiveness was a second chance at life.

Over the ensuing centuries, debt continued to loom as a threat to everyday people. Laws favored creditors, and the Empire needed to tax its people to pay for its ongoing wars and its leaders' luxurious lifestyles. St. Basil of Caesarea rails against Rome's wealthy in his fourth-century sermon, emotionally describing how their lack of generosity pushed poor families into the harsh decision of selling one of their children into slavery to repay a debt so that the rest of the family would not die of starvation:

> Yes, while the glitter of gold so allures you, you fail to notice how great are the groans of the needy. . . . When they look around inside their hovels, they find only clothes and furnishing so miserable that, if all their belongings were reckoned together, they would be worth only a few cents. What then? They turn their gaze to their own children, thinking that perhaps by bringing them to the slave-market they might find some respite from death. . . . Starvation on the one side threatens a horrible death, while nature resists, convincing the parents rather to die with their children. Time and again they vacillate, but in the end they succumb, driven by want and cruel necessity. . . . And while the parents come with tears streaming down their faces to sell the dearest of their children, you are not swayed by their sufferings; you take no account of nature. . . . They come offering their very heart in exchange for food, and yet not only is your hand not stricken with paralysis for taking profits from such misfortune, but you haggle for even more![4]

It was bad enough that poor families had been reduced to selling off their children, but even more cruelly, the wealthy bargained with them on the price they would accept to sell their child.

Widows and orphaned women who fell into debt faced the threat of slavery as well—specifically, sex slavery. Many poor families sold their daughters to brothels to pay debts, and forced prostitution was the only way for women with no male guardians to pay their debts. Sadly, some of those women fell into debt after spending their wealth and inheritances on the church. During the fourth and fifth centuries, the only people who could release "pious women" who had been forced into sex slavery because of their debts were Christian men or clergy, at the request of the women.[5] It is not until the sixth century under the Byzantine Empire that someone systemically sought ways to help these women out of their sex slavery: Empress Theodora, the wife of Justinian, who herself was an actress and courtesan before becoming the emperor's wife.

First, Theodora offered one gold solidus (equivalent to a soldier's salary for one month[6]) to prostitutes to give them the economic means to start new lives outside the brothels, and even paid five solidi to the brothel owners for every girl and woman that left the brothel for a new life, to give the owners an incentive to release them. This, however, was not enough money for these girls and women to live on, so Theodora took a bigger step, opening up a home near the Black Sea called "the Metanoia convent," where they would be taken care of by doctors, nuns, and other Christian women. There they would also learn skills that they could use in society, like nursing, sewing, and so on. An estimated five hundred women escaped the bondage of prostitution and benefited from this service.[7] For this and for the building of hospitals and other important works that improved the legal status of women in Byzantium, Theodora was canonized in the Syrian Orthodox Church and celebrated on June 28.[8]

Unfortunately for St. Paësia, she lived two centuries too early to benefit from Empress Theodora's service to women like her. A contemporary of St. John the Little, St. Paësia lived during the fourth century while Egypt was a province of the Roman Empire. The section on St. John the Little (also known as St. John the Dwarf) in the Greek *Sayings of the Desert Fathers* (*Apophthegmata Patrum)* tells us St. Paësia's story. We'll read it together here:

> The parents of a young girl died, and she was left an orphan; she was called Paësia. She decided to make her house a hospice, for the use of the Fathers of Scetis. So for a long time she gave hospitality and served the Fathers. But in the course of time, her resources were exhausted and she began to be in want. Some wicked men came to see her and turned her aside from her aim. She began to live an evil life, to the point of becoming a prostitute. The Fathers, learning this, were deeply grieved, and calling Abba John the Dwarf said to him, 'We have learnt that this sister is living an evil life. While she could, she gave us charity, so now it is our turn to offer her charity and to go to her assistance. Go to see her then, and according to the wisdom which God has given you, put things right for her.'

We find out here that Paësia used her inheritance from her parents to provide charity and hospitality to the monks of Scetis, who likely traveled to the city to sell their baskets, or perhaps planned to take a longer pilgrimage and used her home as a resting point. When she fell into debt, "some wicked men came to see her and turned her aside from her aim." Those "wicked men" were likely the pimps that traveled the empire in search of families in debt and convince them to sell their young daughters (and sometimes sons) into sex slavery, earning a percentage of the child's sale.[9] The Fathers in Scetis learned of Paësia, and although the text doesn't tell us this, it is likely that she may have been the one to send word for their help since, as mentioned above, the law allowed for clergy to help women like her *at their request*. Tellingly, the fathers used the phrase "put things right for her" when they asked St. John the Little to "go to her assistance." They didn't ask St. John to "get her to repent of her wicked ways," but to "put things right" where things had gone wrong—she, in her charity, had helped the church, but was forced into sex slavery when her funds ran out. The church would have to make things right again for her in the face of the debtors. Here the story continues,

> So Abba John went to her, and said to the old door-keeper, 'Tell your mistress I am here.' But she sent him away saying, 'From the beginning you have eaten her goods, and see how poor she is now.' Abba John said to her, 'Tell her, I have something which will be very helpful to her.' The door-keeper's children, mocking him, said to him, 'What have you to give her, that makes you want to meet her?' He replied, 'How do you know what I am going to give her?' The old woman went up and spoke to her mistress about him. Paësia said to her, 'These monks are always going about in the region of the Red Sea and finding pearls.' Then she got ready and said to the door-keeper, 'Please bring him to me.' As he was coming up, she prepared for him and lay down on the bed. Abba John entered and sat down beside her. Looking into her eyes, he said to her, 'What have you got against Jesus that you behave like this?'

The "old door-keeper" recognizes that St. John is a monk tries to send him away, thinking he might be there to seek Paësia's charity, which she actually now needs. The door-keeper makes a fair accusation: "From the beginning you have eaten her goods, and see how poor she is now." In other words, the door-keeper blames the monks for putting Paësia into such destitution that she must

Paying Debts: St. Paësia and St. John the Little

resort to prostitution. St. John, in his humility, does not tell the door-keeper he is there to save Paësia, positioning himself instead as someone with the means to pay for services, answering, "How do you know what I am going to give her?"

When Paësia hears there is a monk there to see her, she assumes he is there to seek her sexual services. Sadly, this indicates that perhaps there were some monks who did so; the *Sayings* do tell us that some monks did indeed confess of the sin of fornication, so they might have committed those sins in brothels like these. In fact, Paësia tells the door-keeper that the monks "are always going about in the region of the Red Sea and finding pearls," expecting that this monk, too, might be coming to pay for her services with such pearls. She behaves accordingly, preparing herself and lying on the bed, awaiting the monk to do what others seem to have done. St. John, however, does not use her services, and instead asks her, "What have you got against Jesus that you behave like this?"

Reading this story without the context of Roman debt and tax laws, we would assume, as many have, that St. John was asking her this question because he wanted her to repent of her evil ways as a prostitute. Without understanding that those "wicked men" were likely pimps who made their living off of impoverished women, we might think that Paësia went into this life of depravity of her own choice. Mother Lois dispels these assumptions in her article "Heroines not Penitents: Saints of Sex Slavery in the Apophthegmata Patrum in Roman Law Context," where she writes,

> Stories of prostitutes in monastic literature have common themes.
> All are rescued by monastics: Thaïs is rescued by Paphnutius, Paësia
> by John the Dwarf, and Mary by her uncle, Abba Abraham. . . .
> Their rescuers take great measures to reach them. . . . All rescuers
> know the prostitutes personally because they are in some capacity
> their guardians; otherwise, the benevolent rescuer would rescue all
> the women in the brothel. All the prostitutes leave their brothels
> immediately accompanied by their rescuers; none of them lingers for
> a day or even an hour. All of them, once they leave the brothel, are
> kept in places where their guardians are present. All these elements
> of this common story are determined by Roman laws.[10]

Thus, St. John's question to Paësia might not be a question of why she was living life as a prostitute—he knows why. It might be a question of why she thinks he, a holy man, would come to her asking for these sinful services. Here the story continues:

> When she heard this she became completely rigid. Then Abba
> John bent his head and began to weep copiously. She asked him,
> 'Abba, why are you crying?' He raised his head, then lowered it
> again, weeping, and said to her, 'I see Satan playing in your face,
> how should I not weep?' Hearing this, she said to him, 'Abba, is it
> possible to repent?' He replied 'Yes.' She said, 'Take me wherever
> you wish.' 'Let us go,' he said and she got up to go with him. Abba
> John noticed that she did not make any arrangements with regard to
> her house; he said nothing, but he was surprised.

St. John was surprised, but knowing Roman tax laws, we are not. Paësia's house is probably not her house anymore. It has become a brothel and likely owned by the wicked men who push her into sex slavery so she can pay her debts. The only other possible explanation is that she still owns the home but succumbed to prostitution because she would otherwise lose the home to the debt collectors and, homeless, be forced to work for a pimp in an even worse brothel. Either way, she leaves it immediately when St. John tells her it is "possible to repent." She had no trouble leaving behind sexual sin because she never wanted it in the first place. Like so many women and girls in the Roman Empire, she was forced into this life of disrepute and sought any way to get out of it, telling St. John, "Take me wherever you wish," and getting up to go with him. St. Paësia's story continues:

> When they reached the desert, the evening drew on. He, making a
> little pillow with the sand, and marking it with the sign of the cross,
> said to her, 'Sleep here.' Then, a little further on, he did the same for
> himself, said his prayers, and lay down. Waking in the middle of the
> night, he saw a shining path reaching from heaven to her, and he
> saw the angels of God bearing away her soul. So he got up and went
> to touch her feet. When he saw that she was dead he threw himself
> face downwards on the ground, praying to God. He heard this: 'One
> single hour of repentance has brought her more than the penitence
> of many who persevere without showing such fervour in repentance.'

Paying Debts: St. Paësia and St. John the Little

St. John (and/or the writers of the *Apophthegmata*) cast St. Paësia's story as one of a sinner repenting fervently of her sexual sins as a prostitute and receiving God's forgiveness. Yet the "sin" Paësia commits is actually the sin of her entire society. St. Paësia "falls" into prostitution because she lives in a sinful society that preys upon the poor, exactly as St. Basil describes it. St. Paësia escapes sexual slavery in an empire that institutionalized it to keep itself financially afloat and maintain its social structure. If there is any community that needs repentance like Nineveh, it is the fourth-century Roman empire.

If we say that St. Paësia repented, it is perhaps that she repented of her despair, of believing that it was not possible to return to God after falling into prostitution, even though she had no choice. It is the Roman imperial leadership, concerned with fighting wars and amassing territory, that must repent of its need to prey on the poor to pay its soldiers. It is the Roman elite, intent on keeping society stratified in this way, who need to repent of bargaining for the cost of human lives, as St. Basil admonishes. It is the sex traffickers, the pimps, who need to repent of pushing girls and women into prostitution as a solution to their or their families' debts while pocketing their profits. St. Paësia is a survivor of these predatory ways, not a "fallen woman" salaciously seeking sexual sin, although the society around her that forced her into this position views her this way.

Lest we believe this problem has gone the way of the Roman Empire, let us consider that 50 million people globally were "victims of modern slavery," including sex trafficking—in 2022.[11] Many of these people are trafficked for the same sorts of economic reasons they were in ancient Rome: financially precarious positions, families unable to feed their children. In Kenya, for example, the caretakers of children orphaned by HIV/AIDS are often too poor to financially support them, leaving them susceptible to child labor and commercial sexual exploitation.[12] And lest we assume this happens only in developing countries, the U.S. National Human Trafficking Hotline received over 10,000 human trafficking reports in 2021, which represents only a part of such trafficking, much of which goes unreported.[13] Some of this trafficking includes forcing individuals into being filmed for pornography (sometimes even while drugged or unconscious), which is then purchased and consumed online, driving a multi-billion dollar global market for sexual slavery.[14]

We, too, like the Roman Empire, live in a society where it is possible for people to exploit the poor, and where the poor end up being trafficked because our society has not provided them with other options. We, too, like the Roman Empire, live in a society that thrives financially off the backs of impoverished people by supporting the market for child labor and sexual slavery. We, too, like the Roman Empire, have need of repentance.

In New York City, where I grew up, there are anywhere between 2,000 to 5,000 children under the age of eighteen engaged in commercial sexual exploitation (i.e., child prostitution). A study with 200 of such children found some echoes of St. Paësia's plight:

> Nearly all of the youth in this sample (87%) expressed a desire to exit; however, they also felt that the lack of alternatives available to them constrained their choices to the point where they had very few options (if any) but to engage in the CSEC market in order to survive. . . . . Many youth talked at length about the shame, stigma, degradation, and loneliness they felt. They added that being labeled and stigmatized by their family, peers, and society overall, left them with low self-esteem and self-worth, which often resulted in an inability to leave "the life." Beside the self-loathing they experienced from participating in CSEC markets, one of the youths' biggest dislikes was providing sexual services to strangers, and the risk of being raped or killed weighed most heavily on their minds. . . . Even though the overwhelming majority of youth said they wanted to leave "the life," most did not have a plan for accomplishing it, and many had difficulty envisioning an exit route. Most youth, it seemed, blamed themselves for their predicament, but they also admitted that, with help, they might have a chance to get out, or to at least improve their lives. More than half of the teens said stable employment was necessary for them to leave the CSEC market, followed by education and stable housing.[15]

Like Paësia, they needed to do this work to survive. Like her, they needed employment, education, and stable housing to exit their lives of prostitution, and like her, they had "difficulty envisioning an exit route." These words echo Paësia's question,

Paying Debts: St. Paësia and St. John the Little

"Abba, is it possible to repent?" The youth felt "stigmatized" by "family, peers and society" in one of the most liberal and sexually permissive cities in the world. Imagine the kind of stigma Paësia would face in fourth-century Roman Egypt? What the youth hated most about their jobs in prostitution was the prostitution itself: "providing sexual services to strangers." They are not participating in this market because they enjoy the sin of sexual immorality, but because they see no way to leave.

Now, let us consider how twenty-first-century New York City has a much stronger social safety net for young people like these, and compare it to the absolute lack of such a safety net for St. Paësia sixteen centuries prior. We can imagine how trapped in her life she must have felt, how much she likely despised the sexual sin she had to engage in to survive, and why she immediately left her situation when St. John provided her the exit route.

The sin that St. Paësia turns her back on is the sin of despair. She questions if it is "possible to repent," considering how far she seems to have fallen. On being assured by Abba John that yes, it is possible, that nothing could separate her from the love of God, she leaves with him and meets God that very night. Her story gives hope to everyone who has been exploited, sexually or otherwise, and despairs of any way out. Her story also proves that despite the prevailing norms that prevent a woman like her from reintegrating into society, God has accepted her. This message, that God accepted her despite her past as a prostitute, is repeated again and again in the monastic literature. On St. Paësia and the other women in monastic literature forced into sexual slavery, Mother Lois writes, "The world judged them as sinners and, at best, penitents, but they proved to the world that God judged them as saints."[16]

The saintliness of these former sexual slaves clearly leaves an imprint on St. John the Short. *The Arabic Life of St. John the Little* retells many of the same stories told in the Apophthegmata, but it doesn't tell Paësia's story. Some of his sayings and parables in both the Apophthegmata and the Arabic Life, however, show that perhaps St. Paësia's return has a powerful impact on him, coloring many of his parables and sayings.

In one parable, Abba John tells the story of a governor who meets a prostitute and asks her to marry him if she promises not to prostitute herself anymore. She agrees and marries him. Her old admirers hear of it and try to attract her without getting the governor's attention by whistling to her. She hears the whistles of her former lovers and retreats into the "inner chamber" of the castle, stopping up her ears and shutting the doors so she won't hear them. Abba John compares this prostitute to our own souls, and her lovers to "the passions." The governor or king that marries her is Christ; "the inner chamber is the eternal dwelling; those who whistle are the evil demons, but the soul always takes refuge in the Lord."[17] Here the reformed prostitute teaches us how to withstand temptation—by taking refuge in God.

In another interesting parable, St. John tells of a man with two wives. This man's poverty meant that the wives were "naked," so they never left their homes. However, a festival was taking place in another city, and the man wanted to join the crowds to see what would happen there. To take his wives with him, he made a chest for them, placed them both in it, and set sail on a ship with them to see the events.

> When they arrived at the place, one of them got up out of the chest and gathered together many rags and made for herself a garment with which she covered up her nakedness. She went and stood in the crowd, observing and seeing everything that was happening. When the other wife who was in the chest looked out of its chinks and saw her companion in the midst of the crowd, she said to her husband, "Now do you see this whore and her lack of modesty, how she is not ashamed of these shabby clothes on her in the midst of this gathering?"[18]

Note the language the woman in the chest uses against the other wife. She calls her a "whore" for wearing rags in public, "immodest" for covering her nakedness in shabby clothes. St. John has no patience for this. The woman in the chest is not only blind to her own nakedness while slandering and judging her companion, she also is thus unable to enjoy the festival and see all the people there. St. John then makes the lesson to us in this parable clear: "If we forget our own sins, find fault with our brother, and dishonor God, God will dishonor us."[19]

How many people judged St. Paësia without observing their own naked condition? How many people stayed inside their chests and called St. Paësia a "whore" while she "clothed herself in rags" and left the chest where she was naked? She entered the Kingdom of Heaven the same night wearing her rags, while the rest of the society that judged her forgot its own sins—the same sins that trapped her inside the chest to begin with. According to Abba John, a woman of ill repute can be restored, but a monk that judges a brother is more naked than a harlot.

When we recall that the Greek word for repentance, *metanoia*, means a complete turning around, away from the despair of sin and towards hope in God, St. Paësia and St. John's story is one that calls us all to repentance. It calls all of us living in a society that thrives on the exploitation of the poor to repent of our cold hearts and help create change. It calls all of us who stigmatize those who have been exploited to repent of our judgment and slander and recognize our own nakedness. It calls all of us to examine ourselves and set things right where they have gone wrong, even if it requires humility. And most importantly, it calls all those who have been driven to a life of exploitation to turn away from despair and towards hope in God, taking refuge in Him.

Questions for Reflection and Action:

1. How has your perception of St. Paësia changed after understanding the context of her story? What does her story have to teach us now?

2. What are some ways we can be more active in stopping the current global sex trade and helping people escape sex slavery?

3. How does St. John the Little teach us not to judge others?

Part III
FILLED

The Pilgrim Egeria

It is also worth inquiring why the rich man does not see Lazarus with any other righteous man, but in the bosom of Abraham. Abraham was hospitable. The rich man sees Lazarus with Abraham, in order that Lazarus may convict him of hospitability. For that patriarch hunted out those who were going past and brought them into his own house; but this rich man overlooked the one who was lying inside his gate. Although he had such a treasure and an aid to his salvation, he passed him by every day and did not use in his need the poor man's help. But the patriarch was not a man like this, but quite the opposite: sitting before his door he angled for all those who were going by. Just as a fisherman casting his net into the sea not only draws up fish but often draws up gold and pearls, so this patriarch, angling for men, once caught angels as well, and (the remarkable part) without knowing it. Paul in his amazement at this praises him and says, "Do not neglect to show hospitality to strangers, for thereby some have entertained angels unawares" (Hebrews 13:2). If he had known what he was doing when he received them with such good will, he would not have done anything great or marvelous; the whole cause for praise is that without knowing who the passers-by were, and thinking that they were simply human travelers, he called them inside with such eagerness.

—St. John Chrysostom, *On Wealth and Poverty*, Sermon 2[1]

Therefore affliction is the flower that will yield the hoped-for fruits. Hence let us pick the flower for the sake of the fruit. Let us be persecuted so that we may run, but if we run, let us not run in vain. Let us race towards the prize of our spiritual vocation; "so let us run that we may obtain" (I Corinthians 9:24). What is it that we shall obtain? What is the prize, what the crown? It seems to me that what we hope is nothing else but the Lord Himself. For He Himself is the Judge of those who fight, and the crown of those who win. He it is who distributes the inheritance, He Himself is the goodly inheritance. He is the portion and the giver of the portion. He makes rich and is Himself the riches. He shows you the treasure and is Himself your treasure.

—St. Gregory of Nyssa, *Sermons on the Beatitudes*, Sermon 8[2]

CHAPTER EIGHT

NEW EYES: TAMAR AND TOBIT

S cripture names four individuals in the book of Genesis as righteous: Abel, Noah, Abraham, and Tamar. Our childhood Sunday school teachers taught us all about Abel, Noah, and Abraham, but they probably skipped Tamar. Our children's Bibles don't include her story either, and even those who have read the entire Bible often forget her two-chapter interlude in the longer and more well-known story of Joseph and his brothers. Yet Judah, the father of the great tribe of Judah, called her "more righteous than he." And Tamar—not Eve, not Elizabeth, not Mary the Mother of God—is the first woman to be named in the New Testament.

Judah was Tamar's father-in-law, yet he became the father of Tamar's twin boys when she disguised herself as a prostitute to get him to sleep with her. We can see how this would be a difficult story to illustrate in a children's Bible. Tamar had married two of Judah's sons, Er and Onan. Er "was wicked in the sight of the Lord, and the Lord killed him," according to Genesis 38:7, before giving Tamar a child. Then, as was the custom, Judah told his second son, Onan, to marry Tamar so that he could give his dead brother an heir. This was known as "Levirate marriage."[1] Onan, however, knowing that a child of Tamar's would be his brother's heir and thus reduce his own share of the inheritance,[2] spilled his semen before he could impregnate her. Displeased with Onan for spilling his seed instead of getting Tamar pregnant, God strikes down Onan, too. Now we can also see why this story was a bit too complicated for our Sunday school teachers.

Judah has a third son, Shelah, who, according to Levirate law, should then be given to Tamar to give his dead oldest brother an heir. Judah, however, either isn't aware or doesn't believe that his two older sons died because of their wickedness and thinks instead that Tamar is "a lethal woman" and thus to blame for their deaths.[3] So, he tells Tamar to go live in her father's house until Shelah is old enough to marry her, saying, likely to himself, "Lest he also die like his brothers" (38:11).

Tamar goes to live with her father until Shelah grows up, but our Biblical narrator makes it clear that Judah does not intend to marry his youngest son to her. Like St. Paësia, Tamar is now stuck in a situation she can't escape. She has no children by either of her first two marriages, and she cannot marry again except to Shelah. The only other person besides Shelah who could carry out the Levirate marriage obligation is Judah himself. Judah could also have declared Tamar a widow and set her free to marry again outside of his family. Middle Assyrian laws attest to these Near Eastern customs of Levirate marriage.[4]

Judah, however, does not set Tamar free, but leaves her stuck in this strange position where she cannot remarry, but also where the two people who could perform the Levirate marriage obligation refuse to conduct it. This situation seems ideal for Judah: his youngest son is safe from a "lethal woman," and at her father's house, Tamar is out of sight, out of mind. If we've read the previous chapter (Genesis 37), we would recognize Judah's pattern of behavior, because he did something similar to his own brother Joseph. He did not want Joseph around any more than his other brothers did, but he also didn't want to leave him to die, so he and his brothers sold Joseph as a slave to traveling Midianites on their way to Egypt.

The situation, however, is no more ideal for Tamar than it was for Joseph. Out of sight and out of mind, Tamar must live with the stigma of being a barren woman, a harsh punishment for a woman in the ancient world for a crime she didn't commit. In the ancient world, children were a sign of blessing from God, and barrenness a sign of rejection by God. Women whose husbands died before they could bear children were left in socially and financially precarious positions.[5]

Yet Tamar, like Joseph, is not completely out of sight. God sees her and opens the door for her to shake off her stigma and receive a double blessing. When Tamar hears that Judah's wife has died and that he has gone to see his sheep shearers at Timnah, she devises a plan. As St. Ephrem the Syrian points out, she wants the blessing of children, and she means to get it.[6] She goes to the roadside where Judah will be returning from his sheep-shearing, covering herself with a veil so he will not recognize her. At the roadside Judah assumes her to be a prostitute and asks for her services, promising her a young goat. So she asks him for his signet, cord, and staff as a pledge until she receives her payment. He gives them to her then lies with her, unwittingly fulfilling the Levirate marriage obligation. Tamar knows this, Judah does not. This liaison gets Tamar pregnant—with twins!

When Judah gets back to his flocks, he sends his friend with the young goat to deliver to the prostitute on the side of the road as he promised, and to retrieve the pledge he had left her. The friend cannot find her despite asking around. When he returns to Judah with the news, Judah decides to let the prostitute keep his pledge rather than attract attention trying to find her.

Three months later, when Judah hears that Tamar is pregnant, he orders her to be brought to him so she can be burnt to death as an adulteress. So Tamar shows him his signet, cord, and staff, telling him the father is the owner of those items. This is a moment of great risk for Tamar, because Judah could simply deny that they belong to him, and with his word against hers in the ancient Middle East, his would certainly prevail. However, as St. John Chrysostom points out, Judah admits his sin.[7] He acknowledges that the items are his, and thus he is the father of Tamar's twins. Tamar is not an adulteress, but in fact, "She has been more righteous than I, because I did not give her to Shelah my son" (38:26). True to the rules of Levirate marriage, Judah never sleeps with Tamar again. Tamar eventually gives birth to her twin boys, receiving a double blessing.

We will have only heard Tamar's name in church if we paid attention during the reading of Matthew 1, the genealogy of Jesus Christ, during the Nativity season. Four women are mentioned out of the forty-two generations Matthew lists: Tamar, Rahab, Ruth, and Bathsheba. As author David Lamb points out, the first woman named in the New Testament is not the Mother of God St. Mary, nor is it Eve: it is the righteous Tamar.[8] Tamar's name, in fact, comes directly after the great patriarchs: Abraham begot Isaac, Isaac begot Jacob, Jacob begot Judah and his brothers, and Judah begot Perez and Zerah by Tamar. Tamar's son Perez becomes the six times great-grandfather to King David. Tamar's insistence on carrying an heir to Judah makes her an earthly ancestor of Jesus Christ himself.

Tamar's righteousness lies in her ability to see what Judah refused to see. Judah saw a lethal woman, the cause of the deaths of his two older sons and an inconvenient problem for his family. Tamar saw that it was God's hand that brought down her first two husbands, and that if she did not stand up for her rights, she would bear their punishment, too, when what she actually deserved was the blessing of children. One rabbinic tradition interprets this to mean that Tamar had prophetic foresight; according to this tradition, when Tamar became pregnant she made no effort to hide it, instead patting her stomach, saying, "I am pregnant with kings and redeemers."[9]

Tamar's righteousness lies in her willingness to play a part in God's great economy of salvation, even at great risk to herself. If she did have prophetic foresight, then something or someone told her that she needed to bear the seed of the tribe of Judah, from which would come kings, prophets, and eventually, the Messiah himself. We know of another woman who showed this willingness at a similar risk to herself—the Mother of God, St. Mary. Both Tamar and Mary risked a pregnancy that could get them killed, and both of those pregnancies led to the salvation of mankind.

Tamar's righteousness changed Judah, too. Judah had already sold his brother Joseph as a slave by the time he encountered Tamar, and as we discussed above, he dealt with his Tamar problem the way he dealt with his Joseph problem: out of sight, out of mind. Yet when Tamar confronts him with his pledge, Judah recognizes his wrongdoing and calls her more righteous than he. By the time Judah meets the governor of Egypt without realizing that he is Joseph his brother, Judah has completely transformed. When Joseph insists on keeping Benjamin with him in Egypt, Judah is the brother out of all the others who offers to stay with Joseph as his slave rather than leave Benjamin behind in Egypt and devastate his father. When Judah offers himself, his words overcome the governor of Egypt, who finally reveals himself as his brother Joseph. Pre-Tamar Judah is self-seeking and pompous; post-Tamar Judah is self-sacrificing and humble. Tamar has taught Judah righteousness, and his righteous behavior in Egypt triggers the reconciliation of Jacob's twelve sons. Joseph's words can just as easily be said by Tamar: "But as for you, you meant evil against me; but God meant it for good" (Genesis 50:20). The evil dealt to Joseph led to the saving of many lives. The evil dealt to Tamar led to the salvation of mankind.

When we delve deeply into these stories we recognize something important about the character of God: he sees what we don't see. With our earthly eyes, we see how Joseph's brothers' jealousy drove them to deal treacherously with him, but God sees how Joseph will rise to a position of power and use it to save many lives during famine. With our earthly eyes, we see Tamar as a prostitute, but God sees her as the one through whom "the mystery of the incarnation of our Savior is again described to us," according to St. Cyril of Alexandria.[10] God is, in the words of Hagar, "the God Who Sees" (Genesis 16:13).

Moreover, through our baptism, God gives us the gift of some of this divine sight. As we mentioned earlier, in the Coptic Orthodox Church, the baptism of catechumens happens not on Bright Saturday (as in the Byzantine rite) nor on Easter Vigil (as in the Armenian and the Roman Catholic rite), but on the weekend before Palm Sunday, usually on the Sunday of the Man Born Blind. To this day, hundreds of infants in Egypt are baptized on *hadd el nassarra* (Baptism Sunday). The link between the Sunday of the Man Born Blind and our own baptisms here are clear. The Gospel reading on this day, John 9:1–41, describes the miracle of Christ giving sight to the man born blind by literally creating new eyes:

> Now as Jesus passed by, He saw a man who was blind from birth. And His disciples asked Him, saying, "Rabbi, who sinned, this man or his parents, that he was born blind?" Jesus answered, "Neither this man nor his parents sinned, but that the works of God should be revealed in him. I must work the works of Him who sent Me while it is day; the night is coming when no one can work. As long as I am in the world, I am the light of the world." When He had said these things, He spat on the ground and made clay with the saliva; and He anointed the eyes of the blind man with the clay. And He said to him, "Go, wash in the pool of Siloam" (which is translated, Sent). So he went and washed, and came back seeing.

Two unique aspects of this miracle stand out. First, most of Christ's miracles happened when people sought him out, asking for healing. This time, Christ seems to have sought the blind man out for healing. Second, while other stories of Christ healing usually involve him only speaking the words, in this healing, Jesus uses his hands. He does not just touch the blind man with them, but he also spits on the ground, makes clay with his saliva, and then anoints the blind man's eyes with that clay. This healing is an act of creation by the one in essence with the Creator. "For by anointing with the clay He makes good that which is (so to speak) lacking or vitiated in the nature of the eye," St. Cyril of Alexandria says, "and thus shews that He is the One Who formed us in the beginning, the Creator and Fashioner of the universe."[11] Following the anointing, Christ doesn't tell the man to show himself to the priests in the temple, as he has asked others to do, but instead tells him to wash in the pool of Siloam. This, St. Cyril points out, is "as an image of Holy Baptism."[12]

Eyes and light are important motifs in the Middle East and North Africa. Listen in when an Egyptian child asks his grandmother for something, and you'll likely hear the Arabic response, *min 3enaya!* These words literally mean "from my eyes," and figuratively mean, "I'll do anything for you, even give you my eyes." She might also respond *hader ya 3ayooni!* Or *hader ya noor 3eeni.* These words literally mean "yes, my eyes," or "yes, the light of my eyes." Eyes represent love, beauty, and the highest value in Middle Eastern culture. People swear "on the life of their eyes," and when someone wants to say, "be honest with me" in Arabic, they won't just say "look me in the eye" but literally, "put your eye in my eye." Eyeliner, or kohl, used for both medicinal and beautification purposes, originated in ancient Egypt, and is still traditionally handmade all over the Middle East.

Eye symbols feature throughout ancient Egyptian religion. The Eye of Horus, representing healing, restoration, protection, and health, came about when the goddess Hathor magically restored Horus's eye after he lost it in his fight with the god Seth.[13] The Eye of Ra was the female counterpart to Ra, the god of the sun, and the tears that fell from it became the first people on earth. This eye became the "all-seeing eye," providing both protection but also judgment if it saw evil.[14] Eyes continue to feature as an artistic motif throughout the Middle East and North Africa.

It's no surprise, then, that the Christian imagery of seeing, eyes, and light resonated with the people of Egypt, and that Baptism Sunday is the Sunday of the Man Born Blind. The Coptic Orthodox baptism liturgy draws heavily on images of seeing, light, and enlightenment. We cannot see Christ, the light of the world, without new eyes. When he gives us new eyes as he did the man born blind, then we can see his light. Then we can go from "darkness into light, from death into life, from sin into the knowledge of truth, from the worship of idols to the knowledge of the true God," in the words of the Coptic Orthodox baptism liturgy.

C. S. Lewis falls short in his famous quote, "I believe in Christianity as I believe that the sun has risen: not only because I see it, but because by it I see everything else." Christianity is not just a light that helps us see. Christianity is not just a lens through which we view the world. Christianity is our eyes. "You may say that we know that God exists, and we are aware that the Light exists," Fr. Bishoy Kamel writes. "I know that you know, but the basic thing is the presence of the eyes which can see the Light."[15] In Christ, we are not just taking on a new viewpoint, a new philosophy, or a new way of living. In Christ, we are a new creation, and through our baptism, we receive new eyes.

There's another Old Testament story about a "lethal woman," one who marries seven husbands, and each of them dies on their wedding night. In the Coptic Orthodox Church, we read this story in the book of Tobit on the Friday before the Sunday of the Man Born Blind. All the lectionary readings on this day point to baptism (in the case of the Old Testament) or urge the catechumens to baptism (in the case of the New Testament). Catechumens were also often baptized on this Friday, ahead of the Sunday of the Man Born Blind.[16]

Blindness and sight feature prominently in this reading. Before delving into it, a note: the book of Tobit is in the Septuagint, the Greek translations of the Hebrew Scriptures for the Greek-speaking Jews in Alexandria, Egypt, in the second century B.C. When the New Testament writers quoted the Hebrew Scriptures, they quoted them in the Septuagint translation. Today, we might hear about Tobit belonging to a group of books sometimes called the "deuterocanonical" books (or, to Protestant believers, the Apocrypha). If the Bible you own is a New King James Version or New International Version translation, you might not find it, but it is accessible on many Bible websites on the internet and is worth reading. I suggest the Catena Bible website.

The book of Tobit brings us back to Nineveh, only it's many years after Nineveh's repentance. Tobit and his family have also been brought to Nineveh unwillingly, only this time it is because of Israel's unfaithfulness, especially that of Tobit's tribe, Naphtali, which, except for Tobit, sacrificed animals to the calf King Jeroboam set in Dan and the mountains of Galilee (1:5). Israel gets conquered by Assyria, and Tobit is among the Jewish diaspora in that city. It seems that not only has Nineveh also gone back to its wicked ways, but also many of the Jews there in exile have assimilated to this new country, "eating the food of the Gentiles," except our narrator, Tobit (1:10–11). In exile, Tobit gave his food and clothing to those who had need, and buried the dead who were killed by King Sennacherib. When some Ninevites reported this to the king, Tobit ran into hiding, and Sennacherib confiscated his home and belongings. But forty days later, Sennacherib himself was killed, and Tobit's nephew Ahikar, the new king's cupbearer, interceded for Tobit, bringing him and his family back to Nineveh and restoring his family to their former wealth (1:19–22).

During the Feast of Weeks, Tobit holds a feast and asks his son Tobias to go out and search for any poor Jews to join them. Tobias goes out in search, only to find the body of a Jew who had been murdered, his body thrown in the marketplace. Tobit immediately leaves the feast to retrieve the body and place it somewhere safe until sundown, when he will bury it. While he is resting outdoors after burying his kinsman outside the city walls, bird droppings fall into his eyes, blinding him. For two years his nephew supports him before moving elsewhere, and then his wife Anna begins to work. Still, they fall deeper and deeper into poverty, until Tobit begins to despair and lifts up his voice to God in prayer.

In a town called Media, a young woman named Sarah has also despaired. An only child, she was married seven times, and each time, a demon named Asmodeus would kill the groom before the wedding was consummated. So she continued to live in her father's house, and even the maids began rebuking her for her status as a "lethal woman." Not only this, but once her parents die, not only will she have no protection from a husband, but she will have no protection as a Jew in a foreign land. Her position is even more precarious than that of Tamar. At this point, like Tobit, she also lifts up her voice to God in prayer.

It seems Tobit and Sarah have raised their voices in prayer at the same time. They each pray these prayers alone, but God sees them, and hears their cries:

> At that very moment, the prayers of both of them were heard in the glorious presence of God. So Raphael was sent to heal both of them: Tobit, by removing the white films from his eyes, so that he might see God's light with his eyes; and Sarah daughter of Raguel, by giving her in marriage to Tobias son of Tobit. (3:16–17, NRSVCE)

With this dramatic turn of events, the rest of the book of Tobit tells us how Archangel Raphael appears as a man and fellow kinsman of Tobit named Azarias, offering to accompany Tobias on an epic and sometimes humorous journey to retrieve some money his father has placed in trust with a friend in Media, where Tobias's uncle also lives, the one who also happens to be the father of Sarah. Tobit tells Tobias not only to retrieve the silver but also to marry his kinswoman.

During the early part of the journey, a great fish flies out of the water and attempts to swallow Tobias's foot. Azarias (Raphael) tells

Tobias to capture the fish instead, an inverse of what happens to Jonah. Yet both Jonah's time under water in the belly of the fish and Tobias's capture of a similar fish contain baptismal imagery. Jonah's three days in the belly of the fish, fully immersed under water, is both a type of Christ in the tomb for three days, but also a type of our baptism, fully immersed under water but then restored to life. Tobias captures the fish and keeps its gall, heart, and liver, all of which will serve as important instruments that save Sarah and Tobit, also symbolizing baptism.

When Tobias reaches his uncle's home and meets Sarah and her family, he quickly turns to the matter of marrying Sarah. Her father, knowing what has happened to her previous seven suitors, attempts to delay him with food, and then explains what has happened to the previous men who tried to marry her. Tobias refuses to eat another bite until Sarah has been given to him in marriage, and so her parents agree, offering their blessing and drawing up a marriage contract.

When Tobias enters the bridal chamber, he burns the heart and liver as incense as Raphael instructed him to do, and the odor is so offensive to the demon that he flees "to the remotest parts of Egypt," where Raphael follows him and binds him. With the demon gone, Tobias and Sarah praise God, and the next morning, rejoicing that they have been found alive, Sarah's parents throw a fourteen-day wedding feast for them.

"This part firmly represents the sacrament of baptism," Archdeacon Banoub Abdou writes. Just as the Archangel Raphael brings Tobias to his kinswoman's house, "so the priest calls the baptized to baptism in order to become a member of the church of Christ." Just as Tobias drives away the demon by burning the fish heart and liver, "likewise the baptized undergoes the Rite of Renouncing Satan before baptism." Just as Tobias asks Sarah to pray for three nights, "likewise after renouncing Satan, the baptized confesses Christ and the priest submerges him in the baptismal font three times in the name of the Holy Trinity." Just as Tobias lives instead of dying after his first night married to Sarah, "likewise the baptized is reborn a second spiritual birth from the water and Spirit."[17]

The theme of baptism and renewal continue when Tobit takes Sarah with him and returns to Nineveh to his father, Tobit. Again, following Raphael's instructions, he takes the gall and uses it to anoint his father's eyes. When he does, the film falls off and Tobit can see again. This anointing is also reminiscent, for the catechumens listening to this reading, of the anointing of holy oil (Myroon) that they will receive after baptism. Archdeacon Abdou continues, "Tobit's regained sight, his joy over his son's rescue, and Tobias' return with his wife all represent the communal joy over the membership of the baptized in the church of Christ."[18]

Tobit's story is fittingly read near but not quite at the end of the fast. For those of us who are no longer catechumens but believers, there is still a lesson for us in what happens to Tobit. We learn right away at the beginning of his story that he does everything right—he follows the law, he gives to the poor, he is righteous in all he does. Yet, something bad happens to him—he loses his sight, while doing a good work! This seems to happen often during Lent. Occasionally we might hear people joke about the things that go wrong during Lent, calling it a "Lenty Lent." In truth, I can name some awful things that have happened to me or my family during past Lenten seasons: a leaking roof, divisions in church, a pandemic, interpersonal conflicts with family or friends, a major car accident, a sewage flood at home . . . I could go on. This phenomenon is so prevalent that you can find t-shirts printed with the phrase "This is a rather Lenty Lent." It seems unfair that things should go wrong during the exact season we are trying to go right, and yet, that's exactly what often happens.

There are two possible reasons for this. First, we might have approached our Lenten spiritual struggle with the wrong mentality. We might have expected some sort of earthly reward for "being good": for giving our alms, for fasting correctly according to all the rules, for praying more. We might have expected that God might grant us an easier, happier life as a result. We might have lost sight of the fact that our reward for this struggle is not an easier, happier life, but a life with God. Things go wrong all year long, but when they go wrong during Lent they might be magnified because we expect a season focused on fasting, prayer, and almsgiving to somehow grant us "good karma" instead of more struggle. Surely Tobit should get plenty of "good karma" for all the good works he has done, yet somehow instead the bird droppings on his eyes make him blind and unable to support his family. This isn't what he deserves, but this is often what happens, even to the most righteous among us. We weren't promised anything different.

Second, we know that when we seek to get closer to God and engage in the spiritual struggle, we are not just struggling against our own passions and weaknesses. There are powers also struggling against us, seeking evil for us rather than good. Temptation Sunday warns us—if the devil has the gumption to tempt Christ himself, he surely will try to tempt us, too. Just as there are saints praying for us and angels fighting for us, there are demonic powers working to break our wills and ruin our good intentions.

While we can't necessarily blame the demons for natural disasters, it is certainly possible that they play some role in how those disasters affect us. While we can't necessarily blame the demons for our own inclinations to sin, we can certainly expect them to take advantage of those inclinations and offer us more temptation. They can most certainly play a role in divisions and interpersonal conflicts, and even in wreaking havoc on the material world around us. This happens to Sarah. A literal demon with a name kills all the men who want to marry her, and she has not done any evil to deserve such a fate.

Still, Tobit does receive his sight again, though not by his own power, but by God's help. And Sarah gains a husband, not through her own power, but by God's help. At this point in Great Lent, we should begin to recognize that we will not be able to continue this journey with our own power. Whether we are fighting against our own weaknesses and passions or facing unusual battles from the devil, we cannot overcome either of these without the grace of God.

Tobit's story also shines light on an important link between almsgiving and repentance. Tobit exhorts Tobias to almsgiving in his goodbye speech to him before he begins his journey, and in the end, before he reveals himself as Archangel Raphael, Azarias tells all who hear him, "For alms doth deliver from death, and shall purge away all sin. Those that exercise alms and righteousness shall be filled with life" (12:9, KJV). In an interview on Ancient Faith Radio, biblical scholar Amy-Jill Levine explains that for the Jews in exile in Tobit's time, putting "money into the hands of the poor is like laying a gift on the altar." Almsgiving, an important part of Judaism from its inception, "becomes even more important after the destruction of the temple, because it belonged with repentance and a variety of other mechanisms to deal with sin without animal sacrifice."[19] Ben Sirach's proverbial analogy also makes this connection, even while prophetically pointing to baptism: "As water extinguishes a blazing fire: so almsgiving atones for sin" (3:30, NRSVCE).

This brings us back full circle to where we began together, when we started our preparation for Lent with repentance and almsgiving. As we approach Holy Week, when we commemorate the week that led to Christ's betrayal, last supper, and crucifixion, we remember that we don't "atone for sin through almsgiving" or through animal sacrifice, because Christ himself in his infinite love has atoned for our sin instead.

Our ongoing repentance and almsgiving, now, take on a different meaning. Through our baptism, we have been made children of God, heirs of the promise by adoption:

> For as many as are led by the Spirit of God, these are sons of God. For you did not receive the spirit of bondage again to fear, but you received the Spirit of adoption by whom we cry out, "Abba, Father." The Spirit Himself bears witness with our spirit that we are children of God, and if children, then heirs—heirs of God and joint heirs with Christ, if indeed we suffer with Him, that we may also be glorified together. (Romans 8:14–17)

Before our baptism, we were born slaves, captive to sin, but after our baptism, we become "heirs to the life of our Lord Jesus Christ."[20] As heirs, we repent because we recognize that our sins have displeased God, and we need to return to him as beloved children to their father. When we give now, when we do any good works, we do them because "the love of Christ compels us" (2 Corinthians 5:14). When we give to others we are giving to Christ (Matthew 25). When we give, we are not giving what belongs to us, but what God has given us. When we give, we are offering love from the eternal wellspring that never dries up. And joy is experienced in the giving and receiving of sacrificial love.

QUESTIONS FOR REFLECTION AND ACTION:

1. What can we learn from Tamar's righteousness?
2. What are some ways we have experienced misfortune like Tobit, despite our best intentions? How does Tobit's story help us?
3. Although many of us have been baptized, how does the theme of new sight, new eyes, and enlightenment apply to us?

CHAPTER NINE

SAVORING: ABRAHAM

On Sunday night, the first night of Holy Week, my then seven-year-old whispered to me, "I feel sad. Everything is dark." The church walls and curtains had been shrouded in black cloth, in mourning. Gone were the palms and crosses that had adorned the church earlier that morning for Palm Sunday. We could almost touch the hushed quietness of the sanctuary.

My gut reaction as a mother to a young child was to relieve his sorrow by reminding him that the Resurrection and all its jubilation was just a few days away. But I stopped myself. We had just read this prophecy: "The vine is dried up, and the fig-trees are become few; the pomegranate, and palm-tree, and apple, and all trees of the field are dried up: for the sons of men have abolished joy" (Joel 1:12, Septuagint). There is a reason for the darkness shrouding the church, a reason for the mournful tones of our hymns. We are supposed to be sad. We have much to mourn. In the words of the prophet Joel, we have abolished joy.

So we mourn as the prophet mourned. We mourn for how far we as humans have fallen. We mourn for the corruption of our mortal bodies. We mourn for our propensity to sin "and fall short of the glory of God" (Romans 3:23). We mourn because sin disconnected us from God and turned us away from him. We mourn because through sin, death entered the world "through the envy of the devil," in the words of the Anaphora of St. Basil.

In one historical fiction novel about World War II, the author expertly described the atmosphere in New York City when the US government announced the plan for a major invasion in Europe. The air held a degree of elation and excitement, almost celebration. America would finally do something that might turn the tide on a bloody and atrocious war. Yet even as there was hope, it was tinged with sadness and grief. The road to victory over an immense evil would exact a high price—higher than even those characters in that story would know.

Palm Sunday feels that way too. The Feast of Our Lord's entry into Jerusalem, a major feast, is celebrated joyously, with hymns crying out, "Hosanna! Blessed is he who comes in the name of the Lord!" We process around the church with palms and celebrate the triumphant entry of the King of Kings into Jerusalem. Then, right after this jubilant liturgy, we conduct a rite that might seem a bit unusual to those outside the Coptic Orthodox Church—the General Funeral.

During the General Funeral, the church prays a funeral rite on all the believers. Its purpose is entirely practical. Funerals are not prayed during Holy Week; a believer who dies during Holy Week doesn't get a funeral service. Instead, the believer's coffin stays in the church during Holy Week prayers before burial. Thus, the General Funeral is a funeral service for all of us in case we die during Holy Week. Once a year, we get to attend our own funerals.

As we pray the General Funeral so soon after the celebration of Palm Sunday, the mood in church shifts. The Savior has entered Jerusalem, the promised one, foretold by the prophets. We know that in the end he will conquer death—but it will come at a high price: his own death on the cross. The General Funeral enters us into this moment, into this realization. The cost of victory over death is the crucifixion of the King of Glory.

In one of the Holy Week Gospel readings, Mark 8:27–33, Jesus foretells his rejection by the elders, chief priests, and scribes, his suffering, his death, and his resurrection after three days. Peter pulls Christ aside, objecting to this conversation. Jesus rebukes him harshly, saying, "Get behind me, Satan." Then he says to Peter, according to the King James translation, "thou savorest not the things that be of God" (8:33).

I find the choice of words in the King James Version interesting. Today, we reserve the word "savor" to describe experiencing something enjoyable with all our faculties so as to prolong the sense of pleasure. We savor happy moments, delicious foods, beautiful scents, breathtaking landscapes. Even in its earliest uses, according to the *Oxford English Dictionary*, "savor" has meant "taste, flavor, seasoning, condiment, scent, perfume, enjoyment, and pleasure."

The same word, however, has also been used to refer to "knowledge, intellectual or spiritual benefit."

When Christ says "thou savorest not the things that be of God," the King James translators might very well have meant that Peter had no knowledge of the things of God. But if that was their intention, they might easily have used the word "knowest." And Peter did know some of the "things that be of God," for he had, just a few verses prior, confessed that Jesus was the Christ (8:29).

It could indeed be that Christ wanted Peter to savor the things of God in the earliest sense of the word "savor"—to taste, enjoy, and take pleasure in the things of God. St. John Chrysostom explains that when Christ told Peter, "Get thee behind me," he was saying, "follow Me, and resist not the design of My voluntary Passion."[1] The suffering and death Christ had been describing, however, weren't things Peter or any of us would want to savor. Were we in Peter's place, we might have objected, too.

In our Western culture, we work very hard to avoid discomfort and suffering, even if it could lead to our good. The only context it seems socially acceptable to willingly undergo physical discomfort is when training for an athletic feat—such as climbing a mountain. Otherwise, we avoid savoring anything unless it is pleasurable. Yet Jesus rebuked Peter for wanting to avoid the suffering necessary for salvation, for trying to skip the suffering and go straight to victory and triumph. Rather, he needed to savor the things of God. He had to live the full experience of suffering.

Many people in the world today live the full experience of suffering, often with no end in sight. Many are impoverished and exploited by others' greed. Many are migrating to escape war and violence. Many face genocide, ethnic cleansing, or persecution. Many are unjustly imprisoned. Many face illness after illness. Many nurse broken hearts, weeping for loved ones lost to sickness, disaster, violence, or suicide.

How many of us steel ourselves from this pain, building walls of comfort around us, avoiding the news, even as the world around us weeps?

We savor not the things of God.

During Holy Week, the church urges us to face the pain of those around us. We pray many litanies, remembering those who suffer with no end in sight. In the Coptic Orthodox church, multiple litanies are prayed morning and evening, with the morning litanies each accompanied by a prostration. Developed over time, some during very difficult periods in church history,[2] the litanies include prayers for almost every kind of suffering.

Here are a few of them: prayers against division in the church, prayers for those in sickness, for those traveling, for the farmers and their crops, for those who attend to the needs of the church, for the catechumens, monasteries, hierarchs, clergy, congregation, the poor, the weak, the peasants, "those who are in distress of any kind," those who are in "distress of captivity, or imprisoned, or in exile, or afflicted with unclean spirits and devils."

We ask God to "save us from inflation, plagues, earthquakes, drowning, fire, deportation, sword of the stranger, rising of the heretics . . . from all calamities, tribulations, and miseries." We ask the Lord to "soften hearts with charity towards the poor and needy brethren," for protection for women, to "support widows and orphans" and "give plenty to those in poverty." We even pray that God pay the debts of those who are in debt.

While we walk with Christ through the days of his greatest suffering, we remember all those who are in their greatest suffering and pray for them. During those litanies, each of us as believers should be offering up in our hearts the people we know about who are facing war, imprisonment, poverty, sickness . . . any of the struggles the church remembers in those litanies. We can even silently add litanies of our own. Many, many people live through so much pain, much of it inflicted on them by others. Sin still runs rampant in the world, causing immense grief and suffering. We can do little to alleviate it unless we first face it and prostrate ourselves before God about it. Lord, have mercy.

"It's ok," I told my son. "We should feel sad sometimes." We sat with our sadness, listening to the psalm being chanted, in its long, somber, Paschal tune.

There is, perhaps, no greater demonstration of Abraham's righteousness than the story of the sacrifice of Isaac. This text, Genesis 22, has been read by Christian communities on Covenant Thursday (also known as Maundy Thursday) during Holy Week since at least the fifth century.[3] For Christians, this story has always been interpreted as a foreshadowing of the Father's sacrifice of his Son, Jesus Christ.

Until I understood how this story was a type of Christ's sacrifice, the story troubled me. I could not understand why God would ask this of Abraham, after he waited so many years for God's promise of a son. Why would God then ask him to sacrifice him? Why would God even require a human sacrifice like this? Why would Abraham agree to it?

Because we know the end of the story, we know that God did not require the human sacrifice of Isaac, and in fact, the God of Israel, unlike the gods of the Babylonians, Greeks, and Romans, would never require human sacrifice of his people. We also know that Abraham agreed to it because of his faith in God—a faith so strong that he knew that even if he sacrificed Isaac, God would raise him from the dead (Hebrews 11:9). Many church fathers interpret Genesis 22:5, when Abraham tells his servants to stay at the foot of the mountain while he and Isaac went up to worship, "and we will come back to you," to mean that Abraham still expected to come back down the mountain with Isaac, even though he went up with the intention to sacrifice him.

The story of Abraham's sacrifice portrays Abraham's great faith. More than this, it illustrates to us God's love. Origen of Alexandria points out that when God asks Abraham to sacrifice Isaac, he doesn't tell him to do it right away, but to go "into the high land, to one of the mountains which I shall show you." Abraham had to spend three days on a journey with his beloved son, knowing that at the end of this journey, he would be sacrificing him. "For what reason?" Origen of Alexandria asks.

That while he is walking, while he is making the journey,
throughout the whole trip he might be torn to pieces with his
thoughts, that hence he might be tormented by the oppressing
command, hence he might be tormented by the struggle of true
affection for his only son . . . so that the father might consider the
son in this whole lengthy period, that he might partake of food with
him, that the child might weigh in his father's embraces for so many
nights, might cling to his breast, might lie in his bosom? Behold to
what an extent the test is heaped up.[4]

Abraham experienced this struggle for three days, and in the
end, he did not have to sacrifice his son. Yet God the Father
must have experienced these feelings for his beloved son for the
thirty-three years of Christ's life, knowing that he actually would
sacrifice his Son, his only Son, the one he loved. The test is not so
much, therefore, a test of Abraham's trust in God, but of God's
love for mankind. For God himself would do for us what he did
not ultimately require of Abraham to do for him. His Son, who
knew this too, would ask for this cup to pass from him. Jesus knew
what Isaac did not know, yet he submitted himself to the will of
his Father. "Behold God contending with people in magnificent
generosity," Origen says. "Abraham offered God a mortal son
who was not put to death; God delivered to death an immortal
son for humanity."[5] Abraham's sacrifice of Isaac is not just a
demonstration of Abraham's faith in God for us, but a parable of
God's love for us.

Perhaps Abraham's faith that God would deliver Isaac back to
him stems from two previous experiences, not with Isaac, but with
Sarah. In our meditation on Abraham in chapter 2, I left out a
curious story with a promise to return to it: Abram's visit to Egypt.
In Egypt we encounter an interesting side of Abram—he's afraid
he might be killed by Pharoah and his beautiful wife taken to be
Pharoah's wife, so he asks Sarai to tell everyone she is his sister,
a half-truth since she is his half-sister. Considering Abram is
seventy-five and Sarai is confirmed to be barren, she must look
good for her age, because Pharaoh's princes love her and Pharaoh
takes her into his house, rewarding Abram with many sheep, oxen,
donkeys, and camels for this gift of Sarai.

Savoring: Abraham

A plague then afflicts Pharoah's house, and Pharaoh recognizes somehow that Sarai is Abram's wife, not just his sister. He reprimands Abram for lying to him, but instead of killing him as Abram expects, he returns his wife to him and sends him away, along with all the gifts he had given him. Abram expects Pharoah to be a tyrant but finds him instead moral, refusing to take another man's wife, and generous, leaving Abram with his many gifts despite his half-truth.

Until I started reading Patristic commentary on this passage, I had always assumed that this story demonstrated Abram's weakness. The Scriptures don't hide or embellish the lives of our forebears; they tell of both their good deeds and their grievous mistakes. That is why, for example, we know the story of Hagar and Ishmael. Scripture does not tie the stories neatly into a bow for us or hide Abraham and Sarah's mistakes from us. Interestingly, however, many of the Patristic Fathers comment on this half-truth with sympathy towards Abram. Fourth-century Egyptian theologian St. Didymus the Blind calls it "a clever strategy."[6] St. Ambrose of Milan goes further and praises Sarai's love for her husband:

> She was willing, if necessary, to endanger her own modesty rather
> than the security of her husband. To safeguard her husband, she
> lied, saying that she was his sister out of fear that those who were
> seeking to ensnare her modesty would have killed him as a rival and
> defender of his wife.[7]

To the Fathers, Abram's lie (St. Ambrose said it, not me) demonstrates wisdom and trust in God—that even though he lied to defend his own life, God would defend his wife's virtue. He and Sarai leave Egypt peacefully, richer than when they entered. This would foreshadow the Israelites' similarly leaving Egypt after the ten plagues, with the Egyptians giving the Israelites gold willingly as they walked towards the Red Sea. Abram gave his wife, the Israelites gave their labor—and in turn, God gave them both deliverance.

It is perhaps this foreshadowing that should cause us to pause before asking the literal question plaguing modern readers: why did Abram have to lie in the first place? Why didn't he trust in God? How could this behavior be called righteous? The mystery grows when we read Genesis 20—Abraham tells the same exact half-truth to Abimelech, King of Gerar, with the same exact outcome. In fact, in the very next chapter, God gives Abraham his promised son, at the time he promised.

Another question might also plague modern readers: why is it acceptable for Abraham to give his wife or sister over to strange men? From my perspective, this is not acceptable. He lies and then leaves her alone with people that have the intention of taking her in marriage. This is, of course, happening at a time when men and women married sight unseen. Later, Isaac would take Rebekah for his wife, having never met her until Abraham's servant brought her home. As late as the nineteenth century, noble families married off daughters sight unseen for the sake of political and financial alliances. As we read in the previous chapter, Tobit set out to marry his cousin Sarah without ever having met her. That's not acceptable to me now, but it was acceptable, even encouraged, then.

With the eyes of the Fathers, then, who saw only virtue in Abram's behavior both in Egypt and Gerar, we can only understand Abram's behavior to actually demonstrate trust in God. In the words of St. John Chrysostom,

> Let us all imitate this and never become dispirited or consider
> the onset of tribulations to be a mark of abandonment on God's
> part or an index of scorn. Rather, let us treat it as the clearest
> demonstration of God's providential care for us.[8]

Twice, Abram delivers Sarah to other kings, fearful, perhaps, for his own life, but trusting that God will deliver her back to him. The second time Abram does this, he does so *after* receiving the promise from God about a son, *after* receiving the three angelic visitors. By the time God asks Abraham to sacrifice Isaac, Abraham has already experienced two instances where he has sacrificed his wife, only to have her returned to him untouched, and with riches to boot. Isaac will return to him, even if it means God will raise him from the dead. Abraham's example of righteousness becomes for us a living demonstration of God's faithful love for us.

Savoring: Abraham

On Covenant Thursday, we read the story of Abraham's sacrifice in the ninth hour. Soon after, we celebrate a Divine Liturgy together, the only Eucharistic celebration during Holy Week, when Christ institutes for us his holy sacrament. During the Fraction, the moment during the liturgy when the priest begins to break the bread offering, now the Body of Christ, he retells the story, concluding with this prayer: "God, Who accepted the sacrifice of our father Abraham, receive this sacrifice from our hands in this hour." After this, the congregation eats and drinks from the Body and Blood of Christ. We who are hungry and thirsty for righteousness find it is he who satisfies us. Abraham's faith was counted for him as righteousness, but Christ *is* our righteousness.

> For when you have approached God joyfully, he again gives back to you what you have offered and says to you, "You will see me again, and your heart shall rejoice, and no man shall take your joy from you." So therefore, what you have offered to God you shall receive back multiplied. —Origen of Alexandria.[9]

QUESTIONS FOR REFLECTION AND ACTION:

1. Have you experienced the desire to dismiss the need to sit with sadness, with lamentation? How can we practice this in a way that does not lead to despair?

2. Go through the litany examples in this chapter and note any specific names of people or groups to pray for that fall into any of those categories.

3. What aspects of Abraham's righteousness do you "hunger for"?

CHAPTER TEN

CHRIST IS RISEN! THE PILGRIM EGERIA

We began our Lenten journey together with the story of my pilgrimage to Mount Sinai, where Moses met God and received the commandments. Years later, I would visit another mountain that Moses climbed and spoke with God: Mount Nebo. It was on Mount Nebo that Moses saw the Promised Land he would not be able to set foot on in his earthly lifetime, and on Mount Nebo that he died, although no one knows his burial place. This time, I had a nine-month-old in a stroller with me, so I would not climb Mount Nebo on foot as I had climbed Mount Sinai. Instead, I "climbed" the mountain by car, walking about a half mile of paved walkway to reach the top. That's how most people climb Mount Nebo nowadays.

As with my trek on Mount Sinai in Egypt, I didn't go alone. I had my mother and eldest son (my only child at the time) with me on this trip to Jordan. We had given him the baptism name of Moses, since he was born on the feast day of Moses the Arch Prophet on the Coptic Orthodox calendar. As my mother and I looked upon Jerusalem from the breathtaking view on Mount Nebo, we longed to be able to cross the border into Israel to visit, but for many reasons, it wasn't going to be possible at that time. Having learned my lesson from my friend on Mount Sinai, I did not wallow in that disappointment. Rather, I felt immense gratitude for the sight of Jerusalem from where I stood, holding my son where his spiritual namesake stood thousands of years before. And I felt grateful for the place of pilgrimage I was already in, with its larger-than-life bronze serpent sculpture, beautiful ancient churches, and stunning mosaics.

As do fasting and prostrations, pilgrimage as a spiritual practice unites our physical bodies to our spiritual longings. God is always with us, in every place and at all times, and yet we also sometimes need to go places with our bodies to meet him.

The Israelites made a pilgrimage to Jerusalem at least three times a year to offer sacrifices at the temple. Similarly, when we leave our homes to go to church and participate in worship, we are, in a sense, taking a pilgrimage. To worship God, we no longer need to go to the temple in Jerusalem, for Christ himself told the Samaritan woman, "Believe Me, the hour is coming when you will neither on this mountain, nor in Jerusalem, worship the Father" (John 4:21). Indeed, God is now worshiped all over the world, on mountains and in valleys, in soaring cathedrals and small rented halls. No matter where we gather to worship now, Christ has promised that "For where two or three are gathered together in My name, I am there in the midst of them" (Matthew 18:20).

Still, millions of Christians make a pilgrimage to Jerusalem to visit the Church of the Holy Sepulchre every year. Built in the fourth century on the empty tomb of Jesus Christ, it is a fitting place to celebrate his resurrection from the dead. Pilgrims since the fourth century have taken expensive and often perilous journeys to see the tomb, to touch it, and to pray there. Many others long to make the trip at least once in their lifetimes. I understand this desire. When God became man, he became man at a specific time, living in and visiting specific places with a body just like ours. St. Thomas insisted on touching his wounds to be sure he had risen from the dead. The Christian life is life for the whole person, body, soul and spirit, and pilgrimage helps us experience it that way.

My climb of Mount Sinai became one of many experiences of pilgrimage I have taken in Egypt, a country rich in holy sites and, just as importantly, holy people. It is, after all, the embodied person seeking righteousness that makes the site holy. The empty tomb of Christ is nothing but a rock, but it is a rock that Jesus' body touched for three days. The relics of saintly people might just be bones, but they are the bones of people who can pray for me in front of the Lord Jesus Christ in heaven, because of their righteousness on earth. This is how fourth-century pilgrims saw pilgrimage as well. "Their desire was to make contact with holy people, whether through meeting them alive or by being in the places that they had made holy by their former presence there."[1]

One of the earliest pilgrims to the Holy Land and other major pilgrim sites in the late fourth/early fifth centuries was a Spanish woman religious who decided to embark on this journey. Fittingly, Spain is now the destination site of a popular European pilgrimage route, the Camino de Santiago. The Pilgrim Egeria set her sights on the East, however, and kept a journal of her observations and experiences, not unlike her predecessor St. Perpetua of Carthage. While St. Perpetua's journal told the story of her imprisonment and path to martyrdom in the third century, the Pilgrim Egeria's journal tells the story of her journey and path to Egypt, Syria, Arabia, Palestine, and Jerusalem in the late fourth to early fifth century.

By the mid-fourth century, Christianity had become legal in the Roman Empire, and with that came the rise of two important Christian spiritual practices that fed into each other: monasticism and pilgrimage. Emperor Constantine's mother Helena's own pilgrimages in search of the True Cross led to multiple church building programs by the Byzantine Empire at biblical sites to mark their locations. At the same time, people were starting to hear about these holy men and women dotting the deserts of Egypt, Palestine, and Syria, and taking their own pilgrimages just to meet these extraordinary individuals and communities. These monastic communities, some along the path and some not far from the pilgrimage sites, started to provide hospitality and health care to the traveling pilgrims who needed respite along their journeys. Pilgrimage became another way for Christians to practice loving their neighbors. To this day, many monasteries in Egypt are known to provide a simple meal to any pilgrims who come to visit.

My children still talk about how delicious their simple meal of fava beans, some pita bread, and sweetened hot black tea was during our trip to St. Mina the Wonderworker's Monastery in Marriot, not far from Alexandria. We made this journey to visit with a living holy person we knew there, as well as to visit with the relics of the great martyr St. Mina and the relics of the newly canonized Pope Kyrillos VI. Right outside the monastery as well, we were able to visit the burial places of the modern martyrs of Alexandria.

Not far from the sprawling monastery complex lies the ruin of what once was the pilgrimage site second only to Jerusalem in the early Christian period: the ruin of Abu Mina, where once some springs flowed in the desert with healing properties attributed to the relics of St. Mina the Wonderworker. The newer monastery was built near this site, which is now a UNESCO World Heritage Site. During the fourth and fifth centuries, visitors would flock to Abu Mina to get healing from the waters, or to find rest and shelter on their way to pilgrimage in Palestine further north. We took a pilgrimage in this ruin, learning all about how there once stood a cathedral with magnificent marble pillars, how there was a guest house for traveling clergy and another for lay people to convalesce in. We saw the baptistery and the ruins where the rooms must have stood. We wondered at how grand this place once was. I imagined it teeming with pilgrims seeking rest, retreat, and healing of body and soul.

Pilgrims to Abu Mina often purchased small clay flasks with an image of St. Mina imprinted on them. They would pour water or holy oil in those flasks, seal them, and take them along on their journeys. These St. Mina flasks, some from as early as the fifth century, are now found in museums all over the world, because they traveled with the pilgrims, who held them close to their bodies as relics of their own visits to this place. St. Mina Monastery still produces these flasks, which can be purchased by any visitor.

The popularity of Abu Mina points to the role of pilgrimage as a healing practice. Indeed, many pilgrims visited holy sites asking for healing or miracles. According to church tradition, many of these healings were granted to those pilgrims who showed their faith by enduring the arduous and dangerous path leading up towards their destinations. Yet there might also have been another kind of healing during these pilgrimages: the healing aspect of travel itself. "The road is the best medicine," the abbess says in Eugene Vodolazkin's novel *Laurus*.[2]

Travel, even under the Pax Romana, when everyone could traverse the Roman roads and the Mediterranean waters, held its inherent dangers. Sickness and injury befell many pilgrims, as well as civil unrest and road bandits. Yet, outside of pilgrimage and the stories pilgrims would go home to tell, early and medieval Christian life could be quite mundane, with very little excitement, unless it was the unwelcome excitement of marauders coming to invade their cities. Although physically demanding, pilgrimage provided respite from the mundane. It especially provided such respite for women, for whom pilgrimage was one of the few socially acceptable ways for women to travel and see the world.[3]

Egeria was one such woman. Though not believed to be extremely wealthy, she clearly had, or was given, enough means to sustain a long and comprehensive pilgrimage to the holy sites. She also had permission from her home religious community (a monastery, perhaps, or a looser community of lay women, virgins or widows) to leave for a prolonged period of time. She kept her travel journal for the sisters of her community, whom she frequently called "You, ladies, my light,"[4] and with whom the contents of the journal were unapologetically concerned.

As a result, Egeria has both excited and frustrated historians, theologians, and liturgists trying to understand the things she saw. She has provided scholars with intriguing observations about the Jerusalem Rite that has strongly influenced the liturgical rites of other churches, especially the Coptic Orthodox Rite. Her writing is specifically directed towards her community of "sisters," and thus the information it leaves out can be confounding to readers and scholars looking for data Egeria wasn't sharing, either because it was common knowledge for her or because she just wasn't interested. During her visits to "holy men" or "holy people," she names only one, a deaconess named Marthana. The others are spoken of generally, each person "exceedingly holy," with reputations of righteousness known to all. Yet these descriptions reveal a simple truth: regardless of our individual stories or circumstances, righteousness and holiness look the same.

Righteousness, we can glean from the stories of Abraham, Tamar, St. Abraam, St. Paësia, St. John the Little, and Tobit, is made up of four components: intimacy with God; living morally and uprightly; showing love and care for the poor, the oppressed, the stranger; and acting with honesty and integrity. As we can also see from their stories, not everyone who is called righteous always exemplifies all four of these components. The only righteous person that does is

Christ Jesus himself, the Sun of Righteousness. When we hunger and thirst for righteousness, we hunger and thirst for Christ, and when he satisfies us, he satisfies us with himself.

This is what pilgrims often discovered when they arrived at the holy places they sought out. In her book *3000 Miles to Jesus*, Lisa Deam describes some of the ecstatic spiritual experiences that medieval pilgrims recorded on their arrivals to the Holy Sepulchre:

> Pilgrims no longer just imagined scenes from Jesus's life; they were right there, standing in the place he suffered and died. The very stones spoke of Christ's passion. And pilgrims' bodies did, too, as they wept, wailed, and shrieked.[5]

In the surviving portion of Egeria's travels, she doesn't describe such dramatic spiritual experiences, but she repeatedly offers thanks to God for giving her all that she desired on her journey. "I gave endless thanks to Christ our God," she says, "who was gracious enough to fulfill for me, unworthy and undeserving, my desires in all things."[6] While Egeria does not show much introspection in her writing, her words portray awe, gratitude, holy curiosity, and a responsibility to transmit to her beloved sisters back home all that she had seen and heard. All of these demonstrate that she, too, had experienced God where she had gone, for the experience of God is one that incites all of these things: wonder, thanksgiving, a desire to know more, and a desire to share with others what we have seen and heard.

Pilgrimage to Jerusalem as a spiritual practice would continue into the Middle Ages, after the fall of the Roman Empire. No longer able to travel as safely through a world largely Roman-controlled the way the Pilgrim Egeria could, pilgrims from England, France, and Spain had to take a harsh land journey that crossed over political borders and multiple checkpoints. The greatest and most dangerous obstacle on that journey, Deam explains, was the crossing of the Alps. Many medieval pilgrims lost their lives in that frozen climate, getting lost in snow drifts or buried in avalanches. Yet many still braved the Alps because of how much they longed for the holy place they would near when they got to the other side.

We started our Lenten journey together talking about mountains and likening our spiritual struggle during Lent to a mountain climb. Just as I learned on Mount Sinai, some of us might reach the peak, and some of us might not, but our goal has never been to reach the mountain summit. Our goal, like that of the European pilgrims, lies beyond the mountain. Our goal is to get across and reach the heavenly Jerusalem.

For the later European pilgrims, Jerusalem was the destination, and the road was the means to get there. For Egeria, the road is not more important than the destination on a pilgrimage; the road is part of the pilgrimage. A pilgrimage is not an aimless path of travel—one almost always has their feet pointed towards their destination. However, the road to that destination can prove to be as edifying and transformative as the experience of the destination itself. One only needs to ask Susan Ashbrook Harvey and Robin Darling Young, who, as we described in a previous chapter, embarked on a pilgrimage as fellow scholars and returned from the pilgrimage as eternal sisters. While the ritual that sealed their sisterhood happened at the Holy Sepulchre, it was the road together that grew their spiritual friendship.

Thankfully, for the many of us who have not had the opportunity to visit Jerusalem, or who perhaps might never, we are not limited to that one physical place to participate in a pilgrimage. Holy places and holy people can be found everywhere, if we know where to look, and can be accessible to everyone, regardless of their limitations. In the East, where Christianity was born and developed, it is easier to find holy sites with biblical significance and saintly spiritual people to visit with. As we saw in Egeria's travels, although she spent most of her time in Jerusalem, her pilgrimage included many other places, and she was open to many, many detours. She would visit a place, and then hear about a holy site or a place with holy people, and then set out to visit that place. Pilgrimage does not always follow the plans we set for ourselves. Sometimes those detours turn out to be exactly where our pilgrimage was meant to be headed.

Once, I took an accidental pilgrimage to visit the relics of St. Thérèse of Lisieux. My family and I were traveling back from a visit to

Canada, and when we pass through the Niagara Falls area, we usually like to stop. This time we didn't want to stop and pay for parking at Niagara Falls proper, so we thought we might be able to find a free viewing spot nearby and also look for a restroom. As we drove, I saw a sign for a Catholic monastery and wondered about it. So we decided to see if it might be open at least to visit the bathrooms.

When we went inside, we found that we could enter and see the church. We discovered that this monastery had relics of St. Thérèse of Lisieux, whom my husband knew about but my children did not. We stood before her relics, praying and taking some dried rose petals, secondary relics that we could take home as a memory of our journey. For the rest of our drive back home, we listened to an audio book that told us the story of St. Thérèse's life with excerpts from her autobiography, *The Story of a Soul*. Although we visit Canada often to visit family, this accidental pilgrimage marked that particular trip in a special way. We had added one more saint to our spiritual friends.

In addition to worshiping God in our own churches on Sunday, there are many ways to take a pilgrimage that do not involve international travel. Just like St. Thérèse of Lisieux in Buffalo, NY, we may find that there are churches and monasteries nearby, or a short drive away, with relics we can take the blessings of, or even beautiful sacred art in front of which we can stand in awe.

Pilgrimage to the relics and graves of holy ones might seem morbid to some, but for us as Christians it is a celebration of eternal life, of the "great cloud of witnesses" who have run the race marked out before us. We visit with the relics of the dead because we know that we will see them again, at the Resurrection of the Dead.

A few years ago, I took a short pilgrimage to the Monastery of the Holy Transfiguration in Ellwood, Pennsylvania. I had read the memoirs of Mother Alexandra, written about her time as Ileana, princess of Romania, and I immediately connected with her. Knowing she had founded this monastery and was buried there, I took the opportunity to visit in 2019, right after attending a conference held nearby. It was a joyful visit. I got to dine with the nuns, see some of Mother Alexandra's artwork, and of course, visit her gravesite where I prayed and asked for her prayers. I learned when I stopped at her headstone that nearby, Fr. Thomas Hopko is also buried. I had known him and learned so much from him, attending events at St. Vladimir's Seminary when he spoke and Lenten retreats in New York City churches where he was invited, and I even managed to have him speak on my university campus to our Orthodox Fellowship. Seeing his grave there, too, near Mother Alexandra's, was a tiny and welcome detour. At the monastery gift shop, I bought a silver ring with the words "Lord Jesus Christ, have mercy on me" engraved in it as a memory of this pilgrimage and my connection to Mother Alexandra, and as a reminder to pray my arrow prayers.

Not long after that visit to the Romanian princess turned Abbess, I learned that my first book, *Putting Joy into Practice: Seven Ways to Lift Your Spirit from the Early Church*, would be translated into Romanian. I cannot help but think that Mother Alexandra had something to do with that. I went looking for her, and she found me, too.

Pilgrimage can happen where we least expect it. One of my recent pilgrimages was to Christie's Auction House in New York. How, might you ask, is an auction house gallery a holy place? Well, it happened that for a short time, Christie's had the Crosby-Schoyen Codex on display. This third-century manuscript is the oldest codex—a bound book, rather than a scroll—ever found. Its leaves are papyrus, and its contents are several books of the Bible, written in Sahidic Coptic. Knowing the codex was only on display there for a few days before going to London to be auctioned off, at church we quickly gathered some families and took a trip to go see it.

The environment of an auction house gallery is, of course, not the aura of a holy place. It incites curiosity and commercialism, but rarely prayer. Still, when we gathered to look at the codex and take photos, my husband told us, "Take its blessings, too." This, after all, was a manuscript of Holy Scripture. More, it was likely paged by our own spiritual ancestors during a time of great persecution of Christians in Egypt. Many of the people who turned those pages might have been martyrs or confessors. So we touched the papyrus leaves encased in glass and kissed our hands, grateful, like the Pilgrim Egeria. We would not be able to purchase this holy and ancient book for ourselves, since it is estimated to auction for millions of dollars, but we did at least have the opportunity to see it with our own eyes and touch it with our own hands.

Steven Auth, author of *Pilgrimage to the Museum*, sees New York's Metropolitan Museum of Art as a place of pilgrimage. In his book, he describes how different works of art at the museum repeatedly demonstrate man's search for God in art, stopping at different examples of mostly Western Art to unveil its longing for God, even art that isn't considered "sacred." I can identify strongly with that, as I am often spiritually inspired on my visits to that museum when contemplating sacred art, especially ancient sacred art.

My favorite place to sit quietly and contemplate at the Met is the Temple of Dendur, an ancient Egyptian temple built during the Roman period and transported, in its entirety, to the Met as a gift from Egypt to the US for funding the excavation of several other monuments before they were flooded by Lake Nasser. A little-known fact about this temple, which makes it entirely suitable for Christian spiritual contemplation, is that it was consecrated as a church in the sixth century, its date inscribed into the temple in Coptic.[7] My ancient Egyptian ancestors prayed there. So did my ancient Egyptian Christian ancestors. Excuse me while I give thanks to God for my ability to sit before it right here in New York City, alongside others, strangers to me, but brethren for a moment, in our awe of this sacred place.

What do we do if we cannot make a pilgrimage? What if a physical difference, disability or infirmity makes us unable to leave our places, even to go attend our local church? While there is certainly much Christian literature around pilgrimage within our own souls, I would rather not over-spiritualize what is a deeply embodied practice. Still, as a spiritual practice that helps us grow in our intimacy with God and love for our neighbor, pilgrimage should be available to everyone who desires it. How, then, can I experience pilgrimage if I have physical limitations?

One way to do so is to ask those who are going on pilgrimage to remember us in their prayers at their destination and, if possible, light a candle for us. This is a common practice and was a responsibility of the medieval pilgrims. When the medieval pilgrim Felix Fabri reached the Holy Sepúlchre, he had brought with him a list of people who had asked him to pray for him there, and he took it out and spent hours doing just that. When I go with my husband on pilgrimages to relics of saints in Egypt, I often see him pull out his list of names to pray for and place the list on the relic or the shrine while whispering their names in prayer. When members of our congregation travel to Egypt, he in turn asks them to remember us in their prayers wherever they visit.

Another way to do so is to accept a small souvenir from someone's pilgrimage. Like the dried rose petal leaves at St. Thérèse's relics, or the clay flasks of St. Mina, most pilgrimage sites offer some secondary relic or blessing to visitors to take home with them, and those of us who go on pilgrimage can take a few extra secondary relics to give to those who could not come with us. Small photos of the saint with some spices that had anointed those relics taped to the back are commonly distributed at pilgrimage sites in Egypt. Small vials of holy oil connected with the saint are often also distributed. I have received such gifts from friends who have visited holy places I haven't been to. We can ask for or receive gifts such as this, and hold them in our hands when they make their own pilgrimage back to us.

A third way is to consider those places where we can do pilgrimage. After all, not all pilgrimages require traveling great distances or arduous climbing like Mount Sinai. As I mentioned earlier, there might be places of pilgrimage near our own homes that we can reach. Our visit to Christie's auction house was one such pilgrimage. A nearby museum might have some antiquities on display that are associated with sacred spaces. While not traditionally pilgrimage sites, museums can be spaces for contemplation.

We might also find consolation at nearby churches that we don't often frequent. Once, a visiting friend who had lived in Syria for a time asked me to take her to some Syrian Orthodox churches. Providentially, I live in an area with the highest concentration of

Syrian Orthodox Christians in the United States, and there are three churches within a ten- to fifteen-minute driving distance from me. In one, we ran into a deacon who shared the uplifting story of how that particular church was built. In another, they claim to have a thread from the belt of the Mother of God herself, and it is on display in the narthex for all to take its blessing. The third was quite simply breathtaking in its iconography and architecture, its beauty inspiring awe and prayer. All of these churches, too, venerate modern martyrs who suffered and died for their faith at the hands of the Islamic State of Iraq and Syria. I would consider them places of pilgrimage.

In addition, many pilgrimage sites have begun to address accessibility concerns. The shrine for Mother Irini at the Monastery of St. Mercurius in Old Cairo has wheelchair-accessible ramps. This is in keeping with Mother Irini's own practice. During her lifetime, Mother Irini built two altars inside the monastery specifically so that some of the disabled nuns in her monastery could participate in the Divine Liturgy. Prior to her time as an abbess, they could not access the nearby churches where the nuns would usually pray. I have seen such ramps at other pilgrimage sites in Egypt as well.

Wheelchair ramps are only one aspect of accessibility; I cannot be certain, for example, if those same sites also contain accessible restrooms. And there are other ways to make a sacred space accessible and welcoming to various kinds of limitations. Signs in braille and in multiple languages, for example, with the names and stories of the saints we are venerating in that holy place would make it more accessible to those who cannot read the local language. Those of us who might be in a position of responsibility for opening holy places to visitors might work to ensure that the holy sites are welcome to all different kinds of people. There are some cities along the Camino del Santiago that have actively committed to making their portion of the Camino accessible to everyone. We can look to these initiatives as models, and when we work towards making holy sites accessible, we resemble the four friends of the paralytic man in Mark 2, who, finding Jesus inaccessible, "uncovered the roof where He was. So when they had broken through, they let down the bed on which the paralytic was lying" (2:4). Jesus commended their faith then, and will commend our faith now when we do the same.

When we are incapable of making the physical pilgrimage, Christ comes to us as he came to the paralyzed man at the pool in Bethsaida. In many church communions, clergy regularly bring the Eucharist to those who cannot come to church to receive, either temporarily or permanently, bringing Christ himself directly to us. Not only will Christ come to us, but we ourselves embody the pilgrimage for others. I wrote about this in more depth in the "Visiting the Sick" chapter of *Putting Joy into Practice*. For if those who visit the sick and the disabled are visiting Christ himself, then we who are sick or disabled must accept that we are, at that moment, embodying Christ himself, too. This is a marvelous grace.

Ultimately, if we are Christians, our lives are a pilgrimage. As the Coptic Orthodox Litany of the Travelers says, we are all but "sojourners in this place," our feet pointing not to the earthly Jerusalem, but to the heavenly one. Lisa Deam explains that for St. Augustine, "A life of faith and a way of prayer, as he speaks of it, is a pilgrimage."[8] Our mountain climb together during this Lent has turned, indeed, not simply to a climb, but to a pilgrimage. Our end point, for now, like that of the medieval pilgrims, is the empty tomb, our celebration of the Resurrection of Christ. But this is not our final resting place. In the words of St. Paul:

> Therefore we also, since we are surrounded by so great a cloud of witnesses, let us lay aside every weight, and the sin which so easily ensnares us, and let us run with endurance the race that is set before us, looking unto Jesus, the author and finisher of our faith, who for the joy that was set before Him endured the cross, despising the shame, and has sat down at the right hand of the throne of God. (Hebrews 12:1–3)

Our final resting place is in Christ himself, the "author and finisher of our faith," one who satisfies our hunger and thirst for righteousness. In his presence is fullness of joy.

Christ is risen!

THANKSGIVING

Although writing can seem a solitary act, no book is ever written alone. There are so many people to thank for their love and support in the writing of this book, some of whom might not even know that they played a role! God has blessed me so much in this way.

First, my loving family, for bearing with me as I wrote these words every free moment I got. I thank my husband, Fr. Bishoy Lamie Mikhail, not only for taking the kids to church with him to give me quiet evenings at home to work, but also for finding me answers to all my questions in the Arabic language Coptic Orthodox resources that I could not access with my limited Arabic reading abilities. My children, Mercurius, Mariam, and Abadir, thank you for your patience whenever you asked about something and I said, "We'll discuss it after I finish this book." I know it wasn't easy. And thank you for helping me choose the cover! A special thank you, also, to Mercurius, who doublechecked all the Lent lectionary references with me late into the night to meet my revision deadline. I am both blessed and unworthy to take this pilgrimage of life with all of you.

A heartfelt thanks to every single person who asked me, "When is your next book coming out?" Because after you asked me that, I asked you to pray for me. Your prayers carried me through this. Thank you.

Thank you to my dear friend Allison Backous Troy, who listened with an open and patient ear as I worked out some of the concepts of this book, or just vented my frustrations along the way. I'm so honored to have your words opening the pages of this book!

Thank you to my writing buddy Nicole Roccas, for giving me important feedback during the early stages of writing this book. Your thoughts helped me address topics I would have overlooked, and most definitely improved my writing.

I finished writing this book during a writing workshop and retreat by the Collegeville Institute. I thank Patrice Gopo for telling me about it and encouraging me to apply. I'm so grateful that I was able to use this time to reflect and to finalize this book, surrounded and inspired by the other writing women of faith who led and attended this workshop with me: Roohi Choudhry, Kim Goode, Chichi Agorom, May Ye, Angie Chapman, Jamie Eaddy, Kim Goode, Zat Jamil, Aiysha Malik, Joyce del Rosario, and Vidya Murlidhar . . . your conversations and words of beauty this week have blessed me. Thank you.

Many years ago, Silvia Farag invited me to speak at a Lenten spiritual day for the Coptic Women Fellowship. I chose the beatitude "Blessed are those who hunger and thirst for righteousness, for they shall be filled" as the theme for my talk. That talk would spark the idea for a longer book, delving into how this beatitude is emblematic of our journey during Great Lent. Thank you, Silvia, and many thanks to the Coptic Women Fellowship for granting me many opportunities to speak and share my writing.

I thank Mary Jasmin Yostos, my friend on Mount Sinai who changed my whole perspective so many years ago, and who, through her amazing photography, continues to share her unique perspective with the whole world. You can follow her at @trekkinglens on Instagram.

Sophfronia Scott manages to inspire and mentor me in my writing, even when she doesn't know it. Thank you, Sophfronia, for all you do.

I thank Lillian Miao and Rachel McKendree of Paraclete Press for inviting me to write another book and being open and supportive of the idea for this one. I thank Lexa Hale, Robert Edmonson, and the rest of the Paraclete team for all the important aspects of publishing a beautiful book like this. My words shine more brightly because of the work that you do.

Thank you to George Makary for allowing us to use your beautiful icon on the cover of this book and illustrating the three inside sections. Your art brought this book to life. Thank you, Jaime Rall, for connecting me to George and to Kirollos Kilada in our writing work together. We all have Andrea Achi, Michelle Al-Ferzly, and all the others at the Metropolitan Museum of Art to thank for curating the Africa & Byzantium exhibition that brought us all together.

Thank you to Elizabeth Staszak for taking the time to read

the last chapter of this book through the eyes of a person with disabilities. Your honest and insightful review helped me see what I couldn't see with my limited knowledge and experience, and to write a more sensitive and thoughtful closing chapter on pilgrimage for all of us.

Thank you to Bishop Suriel, Mother Lois, Fr. Daniel Fanous, Fr. Sujit Thomas, Sherry Shenoda, Lisa Colón DeLay, Laura Michael, Dr. Patricia Fann Bouteneff, Mireille Mishriky, Dr. Nicole M. Roccas, Allison Backous Troy, Judith Scott, and Summer Michelle Kinard for taking the time to read and endorse this book.

Thank you to the members of my book launch team, whose efforts will bring this book into the hands of many readers.

Although I have implemented some wonderful advice and feedback from many who have pre-read this book, any errors are my own.

A few saints accompanied me in the writing of this book. Their stories appear inside, but I must thank them, too, for their prayers and supernatural guidance along the path. St. Abraam, St. Paësia, St. John the Little, and the Pilgrim Egeria, thank you, and please pray for us in front of our Lord Jesus Christ.

Appendix A:

A chart of the pre-Lent and Lenten period in various church calendars and traditions

Church Tradition	Ten weeks before Resurrection	Nine weeks before Resurrection	Eight weeks before Resurrection	Seven weeks before Resurrection	Six, five, four, three, and two weeks before Resurrection		
Coptic, Ethiopian, and Eritrean Orthodox	Jonah's Fast/ Fast of Nineveh (M–W)		Great Lent				
			Preparation Week: fasting begins Monday				
Indian and Syrian Orthodox	Jonah's Fast/ Fast of Nineveh (M–W)			Great Lent			
				Eve of Great Lent: fasting begins Monday			
Armenian Orthodox	Fast of the Catechumens (M–F)						
Eastern Orthodox	Lenten Triodion			Great Lent		Holy Week:	Feast of the Resurrection
		Meatfare week	Cheesefare week	Forgiveness Sunday: fasting begins Monday		Coptic: Pascha	Eastern Orthodox: Pascha
						Ethiopian and Eritrean: Faskia or Himamat	
						Indian and Syrian: Hasho or Hashacho	
						Armenian: Avak Shapat	
Catholic		Septua-gesima	Sexa-gesima	Lent			
Anglican and other Protestant				Quin-quage-sima/ Ash Wed-nesday	Quadra-gesima (First Sunday of Lent)	Holy Week	
			Shrovetide (Tuesday–Tuesday)				

The actual dates on the calendar on which Lent begins depends on when each respective church celebrates the Resurrection. During the Council of Nicaea in 325, all the churches agreed that the date of the Resurrection would fall on the first Sunday after the first full moon following the Spring equinox. This means that the churches using the Gregorian calendar (the Armenian Orthodox, the Indian Orthodox, the Catholic Church and the Protestant Churches) for this calculation often celebrate the Feast before the churches using calculations based on the Julian calendar and the

Hunger for Righteousness

Metonic cycle (the Coptic Orthodox, Ethiopian Orthodox, Eritrean Orthodox, Syrian Orthodox, and Eastern Orthodox). Every few years, however, the calendars align and all the churches celebrate together. This will happen in 2025, 2028, 2031, and so on, unless the churches decide to agree on a common date. In the Catholic and Protestant churches, Holy Week is counted as part of the 40 days of Lent, whereas in the Orthodox churches, Great Lent ends on the Friday before Lazarus Saturday. During Holy Week, a separate fast begins on Palm Sunday. Before the fourth century, Lent and Holy Week were separate fasts that did not connect to each other. While scholars differ on how exactly Lent came to be in the Early Church prior to the fourth century, the general consensus is as follows:

In Egypt, a 40-day fast was celebrated after Epiphany to commemorate Christ's fast for us in the wilderness, and the Holy Week fast before the Feast of the Resurrection was observed separately, with a month or two falling between the two fasts. However, the preferred time for the baptism of catechumens in most Christian centers was before the Feast of the Resurrection, so many catechumens fasted three weeks before Holy Week so they might be baptized and take communion on the Feast. Over time, the 40-day fast after Epiphany became attached to the pre-Resurrection fast of the catechumens, to become the Great Lent most Christians observe today.

The East, however, has liturgically maintained the separation between the Lenten fast and the Holy Week fast, with special rites observed on the Last Friday of Great Lent. During the Council of Nicaea in 325, not only did all the churches agree on the date for the celebration of the Resurrection, but they also agreed that the Patriarch of Alexandria would announce the date of the Feast (and the beginning of the Great Lent fast) every year in a Festal Letter. At the time, the astronomers and mathematicians were based in Alexandria, so they would give the Patriarch the calculation that would be announced to Christendom.

For further reading on this topic, see:

Johnson, M. E. (1990). "From Three Weeks to Forty Days: Baptismal Preparation and the Origins of Lent." *Studia Liturgica*, 20(2), 185–200. https://doi.org/10.1177/003932079002000205

Russo, Nicholas V. "Lent." *Brill Encyclopedia of Early Christianity Online*. General Editor David G. Hunter, Paul J. J. van Geest and Bert Jan Lietaert Peerbolte. First published online in 2018. https://referenceworks.brill.com/display/db/eeco

Talley, Thomas J. (1983). "The Origins and Shape of Lent." *Liturgy 4* (1): 8–13. doi:10.1080/04580638309414458.

Many thanks to Fr. Vijay Thomas, Fr. Bishoy Lamie Mikhail, Archdeacon Gebre-Kristos Nicholas Siniari, Deacon Alem Sahle, Summer Michelle Kinard, and the Paraclete editorial team for fact checking this calendar.

Appendix B:
The Great Lent Lectionary of the
Coptic Orthodox Church of Alexandria

This lectionary covers the readings for the seven weeks of Great Lent. The eighth week, Holy Week, has its own separate lectionary. Psalm references appear according to the Septuagint numbering, followed in parentheses by the Hebrew numbering (used in the KVJ, NKJV, RSV, NRSV, NIV, and others).

Preparation Week (Week 1)	
Monday	Prophecy 1: Exodus 2:23–3:5
	Prophecy 2: Isaiah 1:2–18
	Matins Psalm: Psalm 6:1, 2
	Matins Gospel: Matthew 12:24–34
	Pauline: Romans 1:26–2:7
	Catholic: James 2:1–13
	Acts 14:19–28
	Liturgy Psalm: Psalm 21:25 (22:26)
	The Gospel: Mark 9:33–50
Tuesday	Prophecy 1: Isaiah 1:19–2:3
	Prophecy 2: Zechariah 8:7–13
	Matins Psalm: Psalm 22:1, 3 (23:1, 3)
	Matins Gospel: Matthew 9:10–15
	Pauline: Romans 9:14–29
	Catholic: 1 Peter 4:3–11
	Acts 5:34–42
	Liturgy Psalm: Psalm 24:16, 17 (25:16, 17)
	The Gospel: Luke 12:41–50

Hunger for Righteousness

Wednesday	Prophecy 1: Isaiah 2:3–11
	Prophecy 2: Joel 2:12–27
	Matins Psalm: Psalm 24:6, 7 (25:6, 7)
	Matins Gospel: Luke 6:24–34
	Pauline: Romans 14:19–15:7
	Catholic: 2 Peter 1:4–11
	Acts 10:9–20
	Liturgy Psalm: Psalm 24:20, 16 (25:20, 16)
	The Gospel: Luke 6:35–38
Thursday	Prophecy 1: Isaiah 2:11–19
	Prophecy 2: Zechariah 8:18–23
	Matins Psalm: Psalm 23:1, 2 (24:1, 2)
	Matins Gospel: Luke 8:22–25
	Pauline: 1 Corinthians 4:16–5:9
	Catholic: 1 John 1:8–2:11
	Acts 8:3–13
	Liturgy Psalm: Psalm 117:14, 18 (118:14, 18)
	The Gospel: Mark 4:21–29
Friday	Prophecy 1: Deuteronomy 6:3–7:26
	Prophecy 2: Isaiah 3:1–14
	Matins Psalm: Psalm 29:1, 2 (30:1, 2)
	Matins Gospel: Luke 5:12–16
	Pauline: Romans 12:6–21
	Catholic: 3 John 1:1–15
	Acts 2:42–3:9
	Liturgy Psalm: Psalm 12:5, 6 (13:5, 6)
	The Gospel: Luke 11:1–10
Saturday	Matins Psalm: Psalm 118:57, 58 (119:57, 58)
	Matins Gospel: Matthew 5:25–37
	Pauline: Romans 12:1–21
	Catholic: James 1:1–12
	Acts 21:27–39
	Liturgy Psalm: Psalms 5:1, 2
	The Gospel: Matthew 5:38–48

	Sunday of the Kingdom of Heaven (First Sunday, Week 2)
	Vespers Psalm: Psalm 16:1, 2 (17:1, 2)
	Vespers Gospel: Matthew 6:34–7:12
	Matins Psalm: Psalm 17:1, 2 (18:1, 2)
	Matins Gospel: Matthew 7:22–29
	Pauline: Romans 13:1–14
	Catholic: James 1:13–21
	Acts 21:40–22:16
	Liturgy Psalm: Psalm 24:1, 2, 4, 5 (25:1, 2, 4, 5)
	The Gospel: Matthew 6:19–33
Sunday eve.	Psalm 47:10, 11 (48:10, 11)
	Gospel: Luke 6:27–38
Monday	Prophecy 1: Exodus 3:6–14
	Prophecy 2: Isaiah 4:2–5:7
	Matins Psalm: Psalm 39:11 (40:11)
	Matins Gospel: Mark 9:25–29
	Pauline: Romans 1:18–25
	Catholic: Jude 1:1–8
	Acts 4:36–5:11
	Liturgy Psalm: Psalm 28:1, 2 (29:1, 2)
	The Gospel: Luke 18:1–8
Tuesday	Prophecy 1: Job 19:1–27
	Prophecy 2: Isaiah 5:7–16
	Matins Psalm: Psalm 40:4, 13 (41:4, 13)
	Matins Gospel: Luke 12:22–31
	Pauline: 2 Corinthians 9:6–15
	Catholic: James 1.1–12
	Acts 4:13–22
	Liturgy Psalm: Psalm 40:1 (41:1)
	The Gospel: Mark 10:17–27

Wednesday	Prophecy 1: Exodus 2:11–20
	Prophecy 2: Isaiah 5:17–25
	Prophecy 3: Malachi 1:6-4:6
	Matins Psalm: Psalm 17:17, 18 (18:17, 18)
	Matins Gospel: Matthew 5:17–24
	Pauline: Romans 3:1–18
	Catholic: 2 John 1:8–13
	Acts 5:3–11
	Liturgy Psalm: Psalm 17:1, 2 (18:1, 2)
	The Gospel: Matthew 15:32–38
Thursday	Prophecy 1: Deuteronomy 5:15–22
	Prophecy 2: Isaiah 6:1–12
	Prophecy 3: Joshua 2:1–6:27
	Matins Psalm: Psalm 27:9 (28:9)
	Matins Gospel: Matthew 11:20–30
	Pauline: Romans 16:17–27
	Catholic: James 3:1–12
	Acts 12:12–23
	Liturgy Psalm: Psalm 47:10, 11 (48:10, 11)
	The Gospel: Matthew 19:16–30
Friday	Prophecy 1: Deuteronomy 8:1–9:4
	Prophecy 2: 1 Samuel 17:16–18:9
	Prophecy 3: Isaiah 7:1–14
	Prophecy 4: Job 11:1–20
	Matins Psalm: Psalm 115:7, 8 (116:7, 8)
	Matins Gospel: Matthew 15:39–16:12
	Pauline: Hebrews 12:28–13:16
	Catholic: 1 Peter 4:7–16
	Acts 15:22–31
	Liturgy Psalm: Psalm 28:10, 11 (29:10, 11)
	The Gospel: Luke 6:39–49

Appendix B

Saturday	Matins Psalm: Psalm 24:7, 8, 11 (25:7, 8, 11)
	Matins Gospel: Mark 9:43–50
	Pauline: Romans 14:1–18
	Catholic: James 1:22–27
	Acts 22:17–30
	Liturgy Psalm: Psalm 117:19, 20 (118:19, 20)
	The Gospel: Matthew 7:13–21

Sunday of Temptation (Second Sunday, Week 3)

	Vespers Psalm: Psalm 50:1, 9 (51:1, 9)
	Vespers Gospel: Mark 1:12–15
	Matins Psalm: Psalm 56:1 (57:1)
	Matins Gospel: Luke 4:1–13
	Pauline: Romans 14:19–15:7
	Catholic: James 2:1–13
	Acts 23:1–11
	Liturgy Psalm: 26:8–10 (27:8–10)
	The Gospel: Matthew 4:1–11
Sunday eve.	Psalm 40:1 (41:1)
	Gospel: Luke 4:1–13
Monday	Prophecy 1: Proverbs 1:20–33
	Prophecy 2: Isaiah 8:13–9:7
	Matins Psalm: Psalm 31:1, 2 (32:1, 2)
	Matins Gospel: Luke 19:11–28
	Pauline: 1 Corinthians 5:9–6:5
	Catholic: 1 Peter 1:3–12
	Acts 17:10–14
	Liturgy Psalm: Psalm 31:5 (32:5)
	The Gospel: Luke 11:33–36

Tuesday	Prophecy 1: Proverbs 2:1–15
	Prophecy 2: Isaiah 10:12–21
	Prophecy 3: Joshua 7:1–26
	Matins Psalm: Psalm 31:10 (32:10)
	Matins Gospel: Luke 12:54–59
	Pauline: Romans 4:1–8
	Catholic: 1 John 2:1–11
	Acts 27:9–12
	Liturgy Psalm: Psalm 31:2, 3 (32:2, 3)
	The Gospel: John 8:31–39
Wednesday	Prophecy 1: Exodus 4:19–6:13
	Prophecy 2: Joel 2:21–26
	Prophecy 3: Isaiah 9:9–10:4
	Prophecy 4: Job 12:1–14:22
	Matins Psalm: Psalm 26:4 (27:4)
	Matins Gospel: Luke 13:18–22
	Pauline: 2 Thessalonians 2:9–17
	Catholic: 2 Peter 2:9–15
	Acts 28:7–11
	Liturgy Psalm: Psalm 26:7, 8 (27:7 ,8)
	The Gospel: Luke 4:1–13
Thursday	Prophecy 1: Genesis 18:17–19:29
	Prophecy 2: Proverbs 2:16–3:4
	Prophecy 3: Isaiah 11:10–12:2
	Matins Psalm: Psalm 9:11, 12
	Matins Gospel: Luke 20:20–26
	Pauline: Romans 4:6–11
	Catholic: James 4:1–10
	Acts 28:1–6
	Liturgy Psalm: Psalm 9:7, 8
	The Gospel: John 12:44–50

Friday	Prophecy 1: Deuteronomy 9:7–10:11
	Prophecy 2: 1 Samuel 23:26–24:22
	Prophecy 3: Isaiah 13:2–13
	Prophecy 4: Job 15:1–35
	Prophecy 5: Sirach 2:1–3:4
	Matins Psalm: Psalm 15:10, 11 (16:10, 11)
	Matins Gospel: Luke 20:27–38
	Pauline: Hebrews 11:1–8
	Catholic: Jude 1:17–25
	Acts 23:6–11
	Liturgy Psalm: Psalm 15:1, 2 (16:1, 2)
	The Gospel: Luke 11:14–26
Saturday	Matins Psalm: Psalm 129:1, 2 (130:1, 2)
	Matins Gospel: Mark 10:17–27
	Pauline: 2 Corinthians 7:2–11
	Catholic: James 2:14–26
	Acts 23:12–35
	Liturgy Psalm: Psalm 26: 6–8 (27:6–8)
	The Gospel: Matthew 18:23–35

Sunday of the Prodigal Son (Third Sunday, Week 4)	
	Vespers Psalm: Psalm 87:1, 2 (88:1, 2)
	Vespers Gospel: Matthew 15:1–20
	Matins Psalm: Psalm 54:1, 2, 16 (55:1, 2, 16)
	Matins Gospel: Matthew 20:1–16
	Pauline: 2 Corinthians 6:2–13
	Catholic: James 3:1–12
	Acts 24:1–23
	Liturgy Psalm: Psalm 78:8, 9 (79:8, 9)
	The Gospel: Luke 15:11–32
Sunday eve.	Psalm 29:1–3 (30:1–3)
	Gospel: Matthew 21:28–32

Monday	Prophecy 1: Genesis 27:1–41
	Prophecy 2: Isaiah 14:24–32
	Prophecy 3: Job 16–17
	Matins Psalm: Psalm 54:1; 26:7, 8 (55:1; 27:7, 8)
	Matins Gospel: Luke 14:7–15
	Pauline: Romans 8:12–26
	Catholic: James 5:16–20
	Acts 11:2–18
	Liturgy Psalm: Psalm 54:16, 17 (55:16, 17)
	The Gospel: Luke 16:1–9
Tuesday	Prophecy 1: Genesis 28:10–22
	Prophecy 2: Isaiah 25:1–26:8
	Prophecy 3: Job 18:1–21
	Prophecy 4: Sirach 8:1–10:1
	Matins Psalm: Psalm 16:1 (17:1)
	Matins Gospel: Matthew 21:28–32
	Pauline: Ephesians 4:1–16
	Catholic: 2 Peter 2:2–8
	Acts 27:1–3
	Liturgy Psalm: Psalm 16:6 (17:6)
	The Gospel: Luke 9:57–62
Wednesday	Prophecy 1: Exodus 7:14–8:18
	Prophecy 2: Joel 2:28–32
	Prophecy 3: Job 1:1–22
	Prophecy 4: Isaiah 26:21–27:9
	Matins Psalm: Psalm 17:37, 40 (18:37, 40)
	Matins Gospel: Luke 14:16–24
	Pauline: Ephesians 4:17–32
	Catholic: James 3:13–4:4
	Acts 11:26–12:2
	Liturgy Psalm: Psalm 17:17, 18 (18:17, 18)
	The Gospel: Mark 4:35–41

Appendix B

Thursday	Prophecy 1: Genesis 32:1–30
	Prophecy 2: Isaiah 28:14–22
	Prophecy 3: Job 20:1–29
	Prophecy 4: Daniel 6:1–27
	Matins Psalm: Psalm 11:7 (12:7)
	Matins Gospel: Mark 3:7–12
	Pauline: 1 Corinthians 12:31–14:1
	Catholic: James 4:11–5:3
	Acts 4:19–31
	Liturgy Psalm: Psalm 47:10, 11 (48:10, 11)
	The Gospel: Luke 18:35–43
Friday	Prophecy 1: Deuteronomy 10:12–11:28
	Prophecy 2: Isaiah 29:13–23
	Prophecy 3: Job 21:1-34
	Prophecy 4: Daniel 14:1–42
	Matins Psalm: Psalm 27:6, 7 (28:6, 7)
	Matins Gospel: Luke 4:31–37
	Pauline: Hebrews 13:7–16
	Catholic: 1 John 4:7–16
	Acts 22:17–24
	Liturgy Psalm: Psalm 27:2 (28:2)
	The Gospel: Matthew 15:21–31
Saturday	Matins Psalm: Psalm 141:5, 7 (142:5, 7)
	Matins Gospel: Luke 16:19–31
	Pauline: Philippians 4:4–9
	Catholic: James 3:13–4:6
	Acts 24:24–25:12
	Liturgy Psalm: Psalm 60:1, 5 (61:1, 5)
	The Gospel: Matthew 21:33–46

Sunday of the Samaritan Woman (Fourth Sunday, Week 5)	
	Vespers Psalm: Psalm 26:14, 13 (27:14, 13)
	Vespers Gospel: Luke 12:22–31
	Matins Psalm: Psalm 30:24, 23 (31:24, 23)
	Matins Gospel: Matthew 22:1–14
	Pauline: Ephesians 6:10–24
	Catholic: James 4:7–17
	Acts 25:13–26:1
	Liturgy Psalm: Psalm 104:3–5 (105:3–5)
	The Gospel: John 4:1–42
Sunday Eve.	Psalm 31:10, 11 (30:10, 11)
	Gospel: John 4:19–24
Monday	Prophecy 1: Proverbs 3:5–18
	Prophecy 2: Isaiah 37:33–38:6
	Prophecy 3: Job 22:1–30
	Matins Psalm: Psalm 87:2–4 (88:2–4)
	Matins Gospel: Luke 12:16–21
	Pauline: Philippians 2:1–16
	Catholic: 1 Peter 3:10–18
	Acts 10:25–35
	Liturgy Psalm: Psalm 85:3, 4 (86:3, 4)
	The Gospel: Luke 9:12–17
Tuesday	Prophecy 1: Numbers 10:35–11:34
	Prophecy 2: Proverbs 3:19–4:9
	Prophecy 3: Isaiah 40:1–8
	Prophecy 4: Job 25:1–6
	Prophecy 5: Job 25:1–14
	Matins Psalm: Psalm 85:5, 6 (86:5, 6)
	Matins Gospel: Mark 9:14–24
	Pauline: Philippians 2:22–26
	Catholic: 1 John 3:2–11
	Acts 24:10–23
	Liturgy: Psalm 85:17 (86:17)
	The Gospel: John 8:12–20

Appendix B

Wednesday	Prophecy 1: Exodus 8:20–9:35
	Prophecy 2: Isaiah 41:4–14
	Prophecy 3: Joel 3:9–21
	Prophecy 4: Job 28:12–28
	Prophecy 5: Proverbs 4:10–19
	Prophecy 6: 1 Samuel 1:1–2:21
	Matins Psalm: Psalm 54:1, 2 (55:1, 2)
	Matins Gospel: Mark 10:1–12
	Pauline: Romans 4:14–5:5
	Catholic: 1 Peter 4:12–19
	Acts 11:12–18
	Liturgy Psalm: Psalm 85:13, 14 (86:13, 14)
	The Gospel: Luke 13:6–9
Thursday	Prophecy 1: Isaiah 42:5–16
	Prophecy 2: Proverbs 4:20–27
	Prophecy 3: Job 29:2–20
	Prophecy 4: 1 Samuel 3:1–20
	Matins Psalm: Psalm 85:14 (86:14)
	Matins Gospel: Luke 9:37–43
	Pauline: 1 Corinthians 10:14–11:1
	Catholic: 1 Peter 1:2–8
	Acts 21:5–14
	Liturgy Psalm: Psalm 85:17 (86:17)
	The Gospel: Luke 13:10–17

Friday	Prophecy 1: Deuteronomy 11:29–12:27
	Prophecy 2: 1 Kings 17:2–24
	Prophecy 3: Proverbs 5:1–12
	Prophecy 4: Isaiah 43:1–9
	Prophecy 5: Job 30:9–32:5
	Matins Psalm: Psalm 85:9, 10 (86:9, 10)
	Matins Gospel: Mark 12:28–34
	Pauline: Hebrews 12:5–16
	Catholic: 1 Peter 4:15–5:5
	Acts 15:36–16:3
	Liturgy Psalm: Psalm 137:1, 2 (138:1, 2)
	The Gospel: John 8:21–27
Saturday	Matins Psalm: Psalm 64:2,3 (65:2,3)
	Matins Gospel: Luke 15:3–10
	Pauline: Galatians 5:16–6:2
	Catholic: James 5:7–11
	Acts 26:1–18
	Liturgy Psalm: Psalm 142:1, 2 (143:1, 2)
	The Gospel: Matthew 23:13–39

Sunday of the Paralyzed Man (Fifth Sunday, Week 6)

	Vespers Psalm: Psalm 38:12 (39:12)
	Vespers Gospel: Luke 18:1–8
	Matins Psalm: Psalm 101:1, 2, 12 (102:1, 2, 12)
	Matins Gospel: Matthew 21:33–46
	Pauline: 2 Thessalonians 2:1–17
	Catholic: 2 Peter 3:1–18
	Acts 26:19–27:8
	Liturgy Psalm: Psalm 32:5, 6 (33:5, 6)
	The Gospel: John 5:1–18
Sunday Eve.	Psalm 141:1, 2 (142:1, 2)
	Gospel: Mathew 9:1–8

Appendix B

Monday	Prophecy 1: Proverbs 8:1–11
	Prophecy 2: Isaiah 43:10–28
	Prophecy 3: Job 32:6–16
	Matins Psalm: Psalm 37:9 (38:9)
	Matins Gospel: Mark 12:1–12
	Pauline: 1 Thessalonians 4:1–18
	Catholic: James 4:7–12
	Acts 18:9–18
	Liturgy: Psalm 34:1, 2 (35:1, 2)
	The Gospel: Luke 13:1–5
Tuesday	Prophecy 1: Proverbs 8:12–21
	Prophecy 2: Isaiah 44:1–8
	Prophecy 3: Job 32:17–33:33
	Prophecy 4: 2 Kings 5:1–27
	Matins Psalm: Psalm 34:13 (35:13)
	Matins Gospel: Luke 4:22–30
	Pauline: 1 Corinthians 14:18–28
	Catholic: James 1:22–2:1
	Acts 19:11–20
	Liturgy: Psalm 41:1 (42:1)
	The Gospel: Luke 9:18–22
Wednesday	Prophecy 1: Exodus 10:1–11:10
	Prophecy 2: Isaiah 44:21–28
	Prophecy 3: Proverbs 8:22–36
	Prophecy 4: Job 34:1–37
	Prophecy 5: Sirach 10:1–31
	Matins Psalm: Psalm 101:17, 20 (102:17, 20)
	Matins Gospel: Mark 7:1–20
	Pauline: Romans 2:12–24
	Catholic: 2 Peter 1:20–2:6
	Acts 26:1–8
	Liturgy: Psalm 9:11, 12
	The Gospel: Luke 11:45–52

Thursday	Prophecy 1: 2 Kings 4:8–41
	Prophecy 2: Isaiah 45:1–10
	Prophecy 3: Proverbs 9:1–11
	Prophecy 4: Job 35:1–16
	Prophecy 5: Sirach 11:1–10
	Matins Psalm: Psalm 9:13
	Matins Gospel: Luke 20:9–19
	Pauline: 1 Timothy 2:1–3:4
	Catholic: Jude 1:16–25
	Acts 27:16–20
	Liturgy Psalm: Psalm 9:13–14
	The Gospel: John 6:47–71
Friday	Prophecy 1: Genesis 22:1–18
	Prophecy 2: Isaiah 45:11–17
	Prophecy 3: Proverbs 9:12–18
	Prophecy 4: Job 36:1–33
	Prophecy 5: Job 37:1–24
	Prophecy 6: Book of Tobit
	Matins Psalm: Psalm 50:7, 8 (51:7, 8)
	Matins Gospel: John 3:14–21
	Pauline: 1 Corinthians 10:1–13
	Catholic: 1 John 2:12–17
	Acts 8:9–17
	Liturgy Psalm: Psalm 33:5, 4 (34:5, 4)
	The Gospel: John 3:1–13
Saturday	Matins Psalm: Psalm 78:8, 9 (79:8, 9)
	Matins Gospel: Matthew 9:1–8
	Pauline: Ephesians 4:1–7
	Catholic: 1 Peter 1:13–21
	Acts 27:9–26
	Liturgy Psalm: Psalm 31:1, 2 (32:1, 2)
	The Gospel: Mark 10:46–52

	Sunday of the Man Born Blind (Baptism Sunday, the Sixth Sunday, Week 7)
	Vespers Psalm: Psalm 16:3, 5 (17:3, 5)
	Vespers Gospel: Luke 13:22–35
	Matins Psalm: Psalm 25:2, 3 (26:2, 3)
	Matins Gospel: Matthew 23:1–39
	Pauline: Colossians 3:5–17
	Catholic: 1 John 5:13–21
	Acts 27:27–37
	Liturgy Psalm: Psalm 142:7 (143:7)
	The Gospel: John 9:1–41
Sunday Eve.	Psalm 40:1 (41:1)
	Gospel: Mark 8:22–26
Monday	Prophecy 1: Proverbs 10:1–16
	Prophecy 2: Isaiah 48:17–49:4
	Prophecy 3: Job 38:1–36
	Matins Psalm: Psalm 31:10–11 (32:10–11)
	Matins Gospel: Luke 16:19–31
	Pauline: Romans 14:10–15:2
	Catholic: James 2:5–13
	Acts 9:22–31
	Liturgy Psalm: Psalm 85:12, 13 (86:12, 13)
	The Gospel: John 5:31–47

Tuesday	Prophecy 1: Proverbs 10:17–32
	Prophecy 2: Isaiah 49:6–10
	Prophecy 3: Job 38:37–39:30
	Prophecy 4: Sirach 5:1–15
	Matins Psalm: Psalm 37:18, 19 (38:18, 19)
	Matins Gospel: Luke 17:1–10
	Pauline: 1 Corinthians 14:5–17
	Catholic: 2 Peter 3:8–15
	Acts 22:17–24
	Liturgy Psalm: Psalm 50:2, 3 (51:2 ,3)
	The Gospel: John 12:36–43
Wednesday	Prophecy 1: Proverbs 10:32–11:13
	Prophecy 2: Isaiah 58:1–11
	Prophecy 3: Job 40:1–41:34
	Matins Psalm: Psalm 56:1 (57:1)
	Matins Gospel: Luke 14:28–35
	Pauline: Romans 10:4–13
	Catholic: James 1:13–21
	Acts 19:23–26
	Liturgy Psalm: Psalm 50:2, 3 (51:2, 3)
	The Gospel: John 6:35–45
Thursday	Prophecy 1: Proverbs 11:13–26
	Prophecy 2: Isaiah 65:8–16
	Prophecy 3: Job 42:1–6
	Prophecy 4: 2 Kings 6:8–7:20
	Matins Psalm: Psalm 62:1 (63:1)
	Matins Gospel: Matthew 20:20–28
	Pauline: 2 Corinthians 4:5–18
	Catholic: 1 John 3:13–24
	Acts 25:23–26:6
	Liturgy Psalm: Psalm 121:1, 2 (122:1, 2)
	The Gospel: Mark 12:18–27

Friday	Prophecy 1: Genesis 49:33–50:26
	Prophecy 2: Proverbs 11:27–12:22
	Prophecy 3: Isaiah 66:10–24
	Prophecy 4: Job 42:7–17
	Matins Psalm: Psalm 97:4–6 (98:4–6)
	Matins Gospel: Luke 17:20–37
	Pauline: 2 Timothy 3:1–4:5
	Catholic: James 5:7–16
	Acts 15:1–18
	Liturgy Psalm: Psalm 97:8, 9 (98:8, 9)
	The Gospel: Luke 13:31–35
Saturday Raising of Lazarus	Prophecy 1: Genesis 49:1–28
	Prophecy 2: Isaiah 40:9–31
	Prophecy 3: Zephaniah 3:14–20
	Prophecy 4: Zachariah 9:9–15
	Matins Psalm: Psalm 87:2–4 (88:2–4)
	Matins Gospel: Luke 18:35–43
	Pauline: 1 Corinthians 2:1–8
	Catholic: 1 Peter 1:25–2:6
	Acts 27:38–28:10
	Liturgy Psalm: Psalm 128:8, 2 (129:8, 2)
	The Gospel: John 11:1–45

Source for Coptic Orthodox Lent Lectionary references: Archdeacon Banoub Abdou, *Treasures of Grace, Great Fast: Linking the Readings*, St. Mary & St. Demiana Convent, trans. (The Parthenos Press, 2023).

NOTES

[1] Emile Maher Ishaq, "Egyptian Arabic Vocabulary, Coptic Influence On," *The Claremont Coptic Encyclopedia*, https://ccdl.claremont.edu/digital/api/collection/cce/id/1988/download

[2] Fr. Morcos Daoud, "Mountains of the Bible and Their Significance (2)," https://www.stmaryofchicago.org/Article/Details/93

[3] Jim Forest, *The Ladder of the Beatitudes* (Orbis, 1999), 20.

[4] Fr. Bishoy Kamel, *Great Lent and Me*, Yvonne Tadros, trans. (St. Shenouda Press, 2018), 14.

Part I

[1] Benedicta Ward, *The Sayings of the Desert Fathers* (Cistercian, 1984).

[2] Hilda Graef, trans., *Ancient Christian Writers: The Lord's Prayer, the Beatitudes Vol. 18* (Paulist Press, 1954), 122–123.

Chapter 2

[1] The Coptic, Ethiopian, and Eritrean Orthodox churches start the fast a week earlier than the other Orthodox churches because a preparation week starts ahead of the First Sunday of Great Lent. This week coincides with the Eastern Orthodox "Cheesefare Week."

[2] H. H. Pope Shenouda III, *Contemplations on the Book of Jonah the Prophet*. Mary & Amani Bassilli, trans. (Coptic Orthodox Patriarchate, 1993), 40.

[3] Joshua Mark, "Assyria," *World History Encyclopedia*, https://www.worldhistory.org/assyria/

[4] Thomas Oden and Alberto Ferreiro, eds., *Ancient Christian Commentary on Scripture: The Twelve Prophets XIV* (Intervarsity Press, 2014), 141.

[5] Aspasmos Watos of the Fast of Nineveh and the Great Lent.

[6] This is specifically true for the Coptic, Ethiopian, and Eritrean Orthodox churches and generally true for the other Oriental and Eastern Orthodox jurisdictions, with some local variation.

[7] Saint Basil, *Letters*, Volume 2 (186–368), *The Fathers of the Church*, Vol. 28 (Catholic University of America Press, 2010), 224.

[8] Dom Gregory Dix, *The Shape of Liturgy* (Dacre Press, 1945), 104, quoted in L. Joseph Letendre, *When You Give: Ancient Answers & Contemporary Questions* (Ancient Faith Publishing, 2023), 20.

[9] Rachel Pieh Jones, *Pillars: How Muslim Friends Made Me Closer to Jesus* (Plough, 2021), 153.

Chapter 3

[1] Thomas Oden, ed., *Ancient Christian Commentary on Scripture*, Genesis 12-50 (InterVarsity Press, 2002), 2.

[2] Thomas Oden, ed., *Ancient Christian Commentary on Scripture*, Genesis 12-50, 13.

[3] Thomas Oden, ed., *Ancient Christian Commentary on Scripture*, Genesis 12-50, 19.

[4] Jonathan Pennington, *Jesus, the Great Philosopher* (Brazos, 2020), Location 196,9 Kindle edition.

[5] Pien Huang and Rhaina Cohen, "How two good friends became sworn siblings — with the revival of an ancient ritual," *National Public Radio*, April 22, 2024, https://www.npr.org/sections/goatsandsoda/2024/04/22/1245859170/siblings-brotherhood-sisterhood-greece-china

[6] Commentary on Jonah 3:10, Catena Bible, https://catenabible.com/com/5839f013205c248f42e53011

Chapter 4

[1] "The Departure of St. Abraam, bishop of El-Fayyoum," *Coptic Orthodox Synaxarium*, https://st-takla.org/books/en/church/synaxarium/10-bawoonah/03-paona-abraam.html

[2] Zaid Fahmy, "Silencing the Streets: Classism, Fear of the Crowd, and Regulating Sounds and Bodies," *Stanford Humanities Today*, 2021, https://shc.stanford.edu/arcade/interventions/silencing-streets-classism-fear-crowd-and-regulating-sounds-and-bodies

[3] S. H. Leeder, *Modern Sons of the Pharaohs: A Study of the Manners and Customs of the Copts of Egypt* (Hodder and Stoughton, 1918), 269.

[4] Magdy Guirguis, Nelly van Doorn-Harder, et al., *The Emergence of the Modern Coptic Papacy* (American University Press, 2011).

[5] Leeder, *Modern Sons of the Pharaohs,* 282.

[6] Leeder, *Modern Sons of the Pharaohs,* 274.

[7] Leeder, *Modern Sons of the Pharaohs,* 274.

[8] William Barclay, *Following the Call* (Plough, 2021), 51.

[9] Tish Harrison Warren, *Liturgy of the Ordinary* (InterVarsity Press, 2016), Kindle Edition, 81–82.

[10] Warren, *Liturgy of the Ordinary*, 82.

[11] Fr. Tadros Malaty, *Anba Abraam, Friend of the Poor* (Santa Monica: St. Peter & St. Paul Coptic Orthodox Church, 1995).

[12] Sr. Benedicta Ward, trans., *The Sayings of the Desert Fathers* (Cistercian, 1975), 103.

Notes

Part II

[1] St. Shenoute the Archimandrite, "Condemnation of Gesios and all merciless, abusive rich people," *Discourses*, David Brakke and Andrew Crislip, trans. (Cambridge University Press, 2015), 242–243.

[2] St. John Chrysostom, *On Wealth and Poverty*, Catharine P. Roth, trans. (SVS Press, 1981), 89.

Chapter 5

[1] St. John Cassian on Mark 11:23, *Catena Bible*, https://catenabible.com/com /5838fee5205c248f42e52e4a

[2] St. John Chrysostom on Mark 11:23, *Catena Bible*, https://catenabible.com /com/5838fee5205c248f42e52e49

[3] "Saint Gregory Thaumaturgus," *Encyclopedia Britannica*, https://www .britannica.com/biography/Saint-Gregory-Thaumaturgus

[4] Maryann M. Shenoda, "Displacing Dhimmī, Maintaining Hope: Unthinkable Coptic Representations of Fatimid Egypt," *International Journal of Middle East Studies* 39, no. 4 (2007), 587–606, http://www.jstor.org /stable/30069489

[5] Iris Habib el-Masry, *The Story of the Copts Book II: From the Arab Conquest to the Present Time* (St. Anthony Coptic Orthodox Monastery, 1982), 112.

[6] "The Departure of St. Abraam (Abraham), Ebn-Zaraa, 62nd Pope of Alexandria" in *Coptic Synaxarium* (St. George Coptic Orthodox Church of Chicago, 1995), 123.

[7] The Coptic Orthodox Church commemorates this miracle three times during the liturgical year. First, on Hatour 18. Then Pope Abraham added three days to the beginning of the Advent fast to commemorate the miracle. We reread the story again on the sixth day of Kiahk, when we commemorate the departure of Pope Abraham, who was Syrian. This same Pope Abraham is the one who brought to the Coptic Orthodox Church the Syrian practice of Jonah's Fast, three weeks ahead of Lent.

[8] Immigration and Refugee Board of Canada, *Egypt: Al-Tar vendetta feuds; underlying philosophy and principles; areas or groups that participate in it; how Egyptian law addresses it; reaction of authorities to violence committed in this tradition*, 2 March 2004, EGY42420.E, https://www.refworld.org /docid/41501c0615.html

[9] Yigal Bloch, "Blood Vengeance in Ancient Near Eastern Context," TheTorah.com (2022), https://thetorah.com/article/blood-vengeance-in -ancient-near-eastern-context

[10] Englewood Review of Books, https://englewoodreview.org/podcast -episode-68-matthew-ichihashi-potts-and-sophfronia-scott-on-forgiveness/

[11] Englewood Review of Books, Podcast Episode 68.

[12] Denise Uwimana, *From Red Earth: A Rwandan Story of Healing and Forgiveness* (Plough, 2019), Location 2004, Kindle edition.

[13] Jayson Casper, "Forgiveness: Muslims Moved as Coptic Christians Do the Unimaginable," *Christianity Today*, April 20, 2017. https://www .christianitytoday.com/news/2017/april/forgiveness-muslims-moved-coptic -christians-egypt-isis.html

[14] Sophfronia Scott, "For Roxane Gay: Notes from a Forgiving Heart," previously published in *Ruminate Magazine*, June 27, 2015, https://www .sleetmagazine.com/selected/scott_v8n2.html

[15] Rasha Ali, "Five years after Charleston church massacre: How 'Emanuel' reveals the power of forgiveness," *USA Today,* June 17, 2019, https://www .usatoday.com/story/life/movies/2019/06/17/emanuel-explores-power -forgiveness-after-charleston-church-massacre/1478473001/

[16] "Forgive us our trespasses," Search the Scriptures LIVE! Podcast, https:// www.ancientfaith.com/podcasts/searchthescriptureslive/forgive_us_our _trespasses/

Chapter 6

[1] H. H. Pope Shenouda III, *Return to Me: Returning to God,* Mary & Amani Bassilli, trans. (Coptic Orthodox Patriarchate, 2020), 54.

[2] Fr. Alexander Schmemann, *Great Lent: A School of Repentance* (Orthodox Church in America, 1977), 13.

[3] *Ancient Christian Commentary on Scripture*, New Testament Volume III – Luke, 245.

[4] "Exegesis By the Numbers: Numerology and the New Testament," *Perspectives in Religious Studies*, 35 (2008), 25–43.

[5] Fr. Daniel Fanous, *Taught by God: Making Sense of the Difficult Sayings of Jesus* (SVS Press, 2020), 185.

[6] Fr. Alexander Schmemann, *Great Lent: Journey to Pascha* (St. Vladimir's Seminary Press, 1974) 14.

[7] Mary Farag, "Pentaglot Psalter," *Africa & Byzantium*, Andrea Myers Achi, ed. (Yale University Press, 2023), 165.

[8] Coptic scholar Alin Suciu described this bit of lore surrounding the manuscript in a Facebook post about it in 2020.

[9] More interesting data: Among these adults, historically Black Protestants and Evangelical Protestants make up over sixty percent of those who read

Notes

Scripture more than once a week. Orthodox Christians and Catholics make up twenty-five to twenty-nine percent of them (Pew Research Center, 2014, "Frequency of Reading Scripture," *Religious Landscape Study*, https://www.pewresearch.org/religion/religious-landscape-study/frequency-of-reading-scripture/).

[10] Celina Durgin and Dru Johnson, "Is It Time to Quit 'Quiet Time'? Effective Biblical engagement must be about more than one's personal experience with Scripture," *Christianity Today*, March 13, 2023. https://www.christianitytoday.com/ct/2023/april/quit-quiet-time-devotions-bible-literacy-reading-scripture.html

[11] John Breck, *Scripture in Tradition: The Bible and Its Interpretation in the Orthodox Church* (SVS Press, 2001), 73.

[12] Dom Armand Veilleux, "Lectio Divina as School of Prayer Among the Fathers of the Desert," a lecture delivered in Rome in November 1995, translated and reprinted on various websites discussing *lectio divina,* including https://oblatesosbbelmont.org/school-of-prayer/

[13] Catena Bible on 1 Samuel 3:9.

[14] Pat. Arm. 13, 8, R: III, 189, quoted in Dom Armand Veilleux. Other versions of this story exist in *The Anonymous Sayings of the Desert Fathers*, John Wortley, trans. (Cambridge University Press, 2013) and in *The Desert Fathers*, Helen Wadwell, trans. (Knopf Doubleday Publishing, 1998).

[15] John Breck, *Scripture in Tradition: The Bible and Its Interpretation in the Orthodox Church* (SVS Press, 2001), 68.

[16] His Holiness Pope Shenouda III, *The Spiritual Means,* Ramza Bassilious, trans. (Coptic Orthodox Publication and Translation, 1998), 49.

Chapter 7

[1] Martin C. Albl, *Essential Guide to Biblical Life and Times* (Saint Mary's Press, 2009), 6.

[2] Walton, quoted in Roland Obenchain, "The Roman Law of Bankruptcy," *The Notre Dame Lawyer*, Vol III.4, March 1928, 171.

[3] Obenchain, "The Roman Law of Bankruptcy," 174.

[4] St. Basil the Great, *On Social Justice*, C. Paul Schroeder, trans. (SVS Press, 2009), 64–65.

[5] Lois Farag, "Heroines not Penitents: Saints of Sex Slavery in the *Apophthegmata Patrum* in Roman Law Context," *Studia Patristica* Vol 64. Papers presented at the Sixteenth International Conference on Patristic Studies, Oxford 2011, Markus Vinzent, ed., (Peeters, 2013). Lois Farag's monastic name is Mother Lois. Farag is a common Egyptian last name; she and I are not related.

[6] "Imperial Coinage," National Gallery of Art, Washington, DC, https://www.nga.gov/features/byzantine/imperial-coinage.html

[7] Paolo Cesaretti, *Theodora: Empress of Byzantium*, Rosanna M. Giammanco Frongia, trans. (Magowan Publishing, 2001).

[8] "Theodora, the Syriac Empress of Byzantine," https://www.soc-wus.org/ourchurch/St.%20Theodora%20Empress.htm

[9] "Theodora, the Syriac Empress of Byzantine."

[10] Lois Farag, "Heroines not Penitents," 26.

[11] International Labor Organization (I.L.O.), https://www.migrationdataportal.org/themes/human-trafficking

[12] Njue, et al., "Child Sexual Exploitation in Kenya," in Dalla, et al., *Global Perspectives on Prostitution and Sex Trafficking: Africa, Asia, Middle East, and Oceania* (Lexington Books/Fortress Academic, 2011), *ProQuest Ebook Central*, https://ebookcentral-proquest-com.libaccess.fdu.edu/lib/fdu-ebooks/detail.action?docID=1214589

[13] https://polarisproject.org/myths-facts-and-statistics/

[14] Hope Watson, "Pornography-Based Sex Trafficking: A Palermo Protocol Fit for the Internet Age," 54, *Vanderbilt Law Review* 495 (2021), https://scholarship.law.vanderbilt.edu/vjtl/vol54/iss2/5

[15] Meredith Dank, "The Commercial Sexual Exploitation of Children in New York City," *Global Perspectives on Prostitution and Sex Trafficking: Europe, Latin America, North America, and Global*, Rochelle L. Dalla, et al., eds., *ProQuest Ebook Central*, http://ebookcentral.proquest.com/lib/fdu-ebooks/detail.action?docID=1211680. Created from fdu-ebooks on 2024-03-27 01:10:21.

[16] Lois Farag, "Heroines not Penitents," 31.

[17] Benedicta Ward, *The Sayings of the Desert Fathers*, 89.

[18] Stephen Davis, "The Arabic Life of St. John the Little," *Coptica,* Vol 7, 2008, 166.

[19] Davis, "The Arabic Life of St. John the Little," 166.

Part III

[1] St. John Chrysostom, *On Wealth and Poverty,* the second sermon on Lazarus and the rich man, 50–51.

[2] *Ancient Christian Writers: The Lord's Prayer, the Beatitudes Vol. 18.* Hilda Graef, trans. (Paulist Press, 1954), 174.

Notes

Chapter 8

[1] Tikva Frymer-Kensky, "Tamar: Bible," *Shalvi/Hyman Encyclopedia of Jewish Women,* 20 March 2009, Jewish Women's Archive, http://jwa.org/encyclopedia/article/tamar-bible

[2] Frymer-Kensky, "Tamar: Bible."

[3] Aliza Shenhar, "Tamar," Raphael Patai, *Encyclopedia of Jewish Folklore and Traditions* (Taylor & Francis Group, 2012). *ProQuest Ebook Central,* http://ebookcentral.proquest.com/lib/fdu-ebooks/detail.action?docID=1158332. Created from fdu-ebooks on 2024-04-04 19:54:42.

[4] Frymer-Kensky, "Tamar: Bible."

[5] John Byron, "EGLBS Presidential Address: Childlessness and Ambiguity in the Ancient World," *Proceedings of the Eastern Great Lakes Biblical Society and Midwest Region of the Society of Biblical Literature* 30 (2010), 17–46.

[6] *Ancient Christian Commentary on Scripture*, Genesis 12-50, 243.

[7] *Ancient Christian Commentary on Scripture*, Genesis 12-50, 245.

[8] David Lamb, *Prostitutes and Polygamists, https://zondervanacademic.com/blog/tamar-the-first-woman-of-the-new-testament-an-excerpt-from-prostitutes-and-polygamists?utm_source=pocket_saves*

[9] Tamar Kadari, "Tamar: Midrash and Aggadah," *Shalvi/Hyman Encyclopedia of Jewish Women,* 20 March 2009, Jewish Women's Archive, http://jwa.org/encyclopedia/article/tamar-midrash-and-aggadah

[10] *Ancient Christian Commentary on Scripture*, Genesis 12-50, 244.

[11] St. Cyril of Alexandria, Catena Bible, https://catenabible.com/com/57eb0c75b0d44ee10cfabf7e

[12] St. Cyril of Alexandria, Catena Bible.

[13] "Eye of Horus," Encyclopedia Britannica, https://www.britannica.com/topic/Eye-of-Horus

[14] Rosie Lesso, "What is the Eye of Ra?" TheCollector.com, October 31, 2023, https://www.thecollector.com/what-is-the-egyptian-eye-of-ra/

[15] Fr. Bishoy Kamel, *Great Lent and Me*, Yvonne Tadros, trans. (St. Shenouda Press, 2018), 145.

[16] Fr. Athanasius el-Makary, *Som Ninawah wal som al moqada el Kabeer* (Arabic), 2nd edition (El Nobar: 2013), 324.

[17] Archdeacon Banoub Abdou, *Treasures of Grace, Great Fast: Linking the Readings*, St. Mary & St. Demiana Convent, trans. (The Parthenos Press, 2023), 229.

[18] Abdou, *Treasures of Grace, Great Fast*, 230.

[19] J. Miller and J. Bennet, "Dr. Amy-Jill Levine Talks Tobit and Canon Envy,"

Bad Books of the Bible Podcast, Ancient Faith Radio, August 10, 2021. Transcript: https://badbooks.substack.com/p/amy-jill-levine-tobit-canon-envy
[20] Coptic Orthodox Baptism liturgy.

Chapter 9

[1] St. John Chrysostom, *Catena Bible*, https://catenabible.com/com /5735de63ec4bd7c9723b9bc8

[2] Youhanna Nessim Youssef, *The History of the Rite of Holy Week in the Coptic Orthodox Church* (St. Shenouda Press, 2023).

[3] Youssef, *The History of the Rite of Holy Week in the Coptic Orthodox Church.*

[4] Origen of Alexandria, *Ancient Christian Commentary on Scripture,* Genesis 12-50, 103.

[5] Origen of Alexandria, *Ancient Christian Commentary on Scripture,* Genesis 12-15, 108.

[6] St. Didymus the Blind, *Ancient Christian Commentary on Scripture*, Genesis 12-15, 7.

[7] St. Ambrose, *Ancient Christian Commentary on Scripture*, Genesis 12-15, 8.

[8] St. John Chrysostom, *Ancient Christian Commentary on Scripture,* Genesis 12-50, 11.

[9] Origen of Alexandria, *Ancient Christian Commentary on Scripture,* Genesis 12-50, 111.

Chapter 10

[1] Anne McGowan and Paul Bradshaw, *The Pilgrimage of Egeria: A New Translation of the* Itinerarium Egeriae *with Introduction and Commentary* (Liturgical Press, 2018), 46.

[2] Eugene Vodolazkin, *Laurus* (Oneworld, 2016).

[3] McGowan and Bradshaw, *The Pilgrimage of Egeria*, 27.

[4] McGowan and Bradshaw, *The Pilgrimage of Egeria*, 148–149.

[5] Lisa Deam, *3000 Miles to Jesus* (Broadleaf, 2021), 169.

[6] McGowan and Bradshaw, *The Pilgrimage of Egeria*, 148.

[7] "The Temple of Dendur," Metropolitan Museum of Art, https://www .metmuseum.org/art/collection/search/547802

[8] Deam, *3000 Miles to Jesus*, 170.

ABOUT PARACLETE PRESS

PARACLETE PRESS IS THE PUBLISHING ARM
of the Cape Cod Benedictine community, the
Community of Jesus. Presenting a full expression of
Christian belief and practice, we reflect the ecumenical
charism of the Community and its dedication to
sacred music, the fine arts, and the written word.

Learn more about us at our website:
www.paracletepress.com
or phone us toll-free at 1.800.451.5006

SCAN
TO
READ
MORE

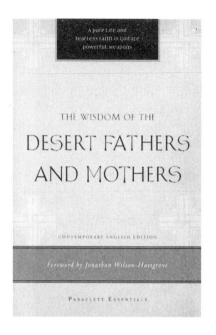

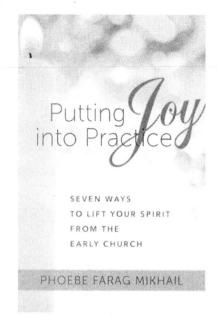

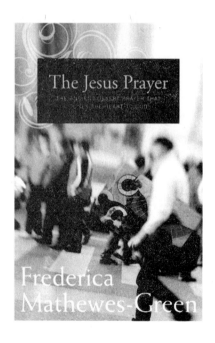